CRIME AND JUSTICE IN OUR TIME

CRIME AND JUSTICE IN OUR TIME

BY MARGARET O. HYDE

FRANKLIN WATTS
NEW YORK/LONDON/TORONTO/SYDNEY/1980

Permission to reprint *TV on Trial* granted by WPBT-TV, Miami, Florida.

Library of Congress Cataloging in Publication Data

Hyde, Margaret Oldroyd, 1917–
   Crime and justice in our time.

      Bibliography: p.
      Includes index.
      SUMMARY: Discusses various types and causes of crime; describes the "typical" criminal; examines the criminal justice systems of the past and present; and explores one's personal responsibility for crime prevention.
      I. Title.
   HV6789.H92   364'.973   79–23806
   ISBN 0-531-04116-6

Copyright © 1980 by Margaret O. Hyde
All rights reserved
Printed in the United States of America
5 4 3 2 1

CONTENTS

Who is a Criminal?	1
What Causes Crime?	7
Cry Help!	16
From Apprehension to Trial	24
"Guilty as Charged!" What Next?	40
Law and Justice in Yesteryear	57
Your Part in Crime Prevention	69
Suggested Reading	79
TV on Trial—The Trial of Ronney Zamora	82
Index	115

To Roxann Marie Russell

*"Is it possible that man can go to the moon
but cannot cope with violence in the street?"*

Remark by a man whose store had been broken into
on forty-nine occasions over a period of two years.

CRIME AND JUSTICE IN OUR TIME

WHO IS A CRIMINAL?

A ten-year-old girl is sexually assaulted.

A teen-age boy tells a bartender he is legally old enough to buy a drink. The bartender does not bother to check and sells the boy several drinks. On the way home, the boy, who is driving a car, is involved in a minor traffic accident.

A girl is invited to a large party at the home of someone she has recently met. She does not go to the party planning to steal anything, but when she is putting on her coat in the bedroom after the party, she sees an attractive pair of earrings lying on the bureau. The temptation is too great. She grabs up the earrings, puts them into her pocket, and leaves with the other guests.

A father stabs his ten-month-old son to death. The mother, who tries to stop him, is cut severely. When the police come to arrest the man, he goes with them quietly. His only remark is one of regret that he did not have time to remove the child's head in accordance with his religious beliefs.

When you read about people like these, you know that

you are reading about criminals. But you may react to each of them in a different way. The person who attacked the ten-year-old girl, for instance, might be considered sick and in need of psychiatric help. The crimes committed by the bartender and the teen-age boy might not even be considered crimes, certainly not serious ones. Perhaps the girl who stole the earrings will never be caught. Perhaps she will never repeat this kind of action. Certainly she does not think of herself as a criminal, though she has read the many signs in department stores which warn that shoplifting is a crime. And, horrified as we may be by the killing of an infant, the murderer in this case seems to have been acting out of some sort of religious conviction.

Each of the above situations involves people breaking the law, committing a crime. But each has special circumstances that prevent it from being an example of a *typical* crime. Not one of these people really fits the picture of the common criminal.

Who, then, does represent the typical criminal? If someone were to ask you this question, what would you say? Would you think of a mugger, a burglar, a murderer? Would you consider a salesman who pads his expense account a criminal? Do you think all criminals are bad people, sinful people, drunks, or disturbed people? Is anyone who has broken a law a criminal in your eyes?

Individuals who break the law for personal reasons are just one kind of criminal. People who misrepresent products in advertising, fix prices, falsify records, or engage in many other kinds of activities known as occupational crime are another kind of criminal.

According to some recent studies, close to 100 percent of all persons have committed some kind of crime or offense, and a substantial portion of these crimes could have resulted in incarceration if the people had been caught and prosecuted.

Obviously, then, there is no typical criminal. Criminals are as varied as the human race. No two are exactly alike, and only a small percentage of criminals fit the picture most people have of them.

In general, the image of a criminal is one of a person who is psychologically unstable, evil, mean, and dangerous. The criminal is often seen as a person who suffers from a "criminal disposition," which cannot be changed. In most television crime shows, the criminal serves a function in the plot, and his or her character is seldom developed. Thus many people who watch television come to think of criminals as alien beings who are part of a make-believe world.

Hard-core criminals, people who are arrested time and again and who actually seem to make crime their career, may fit this image better than most. In an effort to understand why certain people make a "career" out of crime, a psychiatrist, Samuel Yochelson, and a psychologist, Stanton Samenow, studied the male patients at Saint Elizabeths Hospital in Washington, D.C., for fifteen years. Saint Elizabeths is the federal psychiatric hospital for the criminally insane. Their study, later published in three volumes under the title, *The Criminal Personality,* did not really concern itself with the causes of crime as much as with describing the personality of the hard-core criminal in order to discover new ways to deal with it. The doctors concluded that there was a criminal personality type among the men they studied, and they called the composite of this type "C."

C, they said, appears to be a person who is ruled by fears—the fear of being put down by others, of being seen as weak, of getting caught, and of being physically injured. C is excessively concerned with body image and health and cannot tolerate any criticism. C lies as naturally as he breathes. He considers himself a good person because his definition of right is whatever is right for him at the time. C is filled with anger and finds normal life boring. The need to go to extreme lengths for excitement goes hand in hand with a proclivity toward criminal behavior.

Many people who work with criminals have found this study to be valid and useful, but many others disagree that there is such a thing as a criminal personality even among those who repeat serious and violent crimes. These people feel that it is a mistake to think of career criminals as being basically different from other people.

However, even if there is a criminal type—C—then C still cannot be considered representative of a typical criminal, for most criminals are not serious offenders.

Part of the problem in identifying or defining who is a criminal is related to the nature of the society in which we live. By usual definition, criminals are people who break laws. But laws vary from place to place and from time to time. Some laws are even broken unwittingly. This is not hard to understand, considering the number of obsolete or obscure laws which are largely unknown. At various times and in different places, it was criminal to change the oil in a car on Sunday, to print a book, to write a check for less than one dollar, and to have gold in the house. Although it is illegal in some states to paste something on the windshield of a car, other states require motorists to have inspection stickers pasted there.

Interpretation of the law varies, too, as do the punishments for many crimes. A person may be sentenced to a long imprisonment for possessing a small amount of marijuana in one state, while in a different state the punishment would be only a fine. In one state a man who pleaded guilty to manslaughter after strangling a girl and mutilating her body was given a sentence of seven-and-a-half to fifteen years in jail. In another state, or after a different trial, the same man might have been given a life sentence.

Not only do laws, interpretations of laws, and sentences vary greatly, but the offenders who are apprehended, arrested, convicted, and sentenced to institutions also differ, on the average, from the offenders in the general population. The typical adult offender in an institution is likely to be:[1]

poor and unemployed
a school dropout with 8.6 years of schooling (the general population average is 10.6)
over twenty-four years of age
from a broken home
mildly retarded
when employed, working at a low-station occupation
known to have an earlier criminal record
functioning at fifth-grade level
psychologically insecure, with low self-image and little self-discipline

But most offenders, or criminals, are not in institutions. Most of the people arrested do not even go to institutions, and most criminals are not apprehended. The percentage of crimes reported is probably less than fifty. Certainly, one cannot use the above characteristics to describe a typical criminal.

Most persons who are arrested for serious crimes have been offenders before, but relatively few have prior convictions. Since there is a tendency to "forgive" first offenders and "get tough" with habitual criminals, it is not surprising to find that the criminal in an institution has committed a number of crimes. Professor Marvin Wolfgang and his associates at the University of Pennsylvania are famous for their studies on who commits crime. In recent studies, it was estimated that 15 percent of the urban male population between the ages of

---

1. Georgia Committee of National Council on Crime and Delinquency, "Speaker's Source Kit on Crime and Delinquency" (Athens, Ga.: Institute of Government, University of Georgia and WAGA-TV, Atlanta, Ga., 1976).

fourteen and twenty-nine are chronic offenders who account for approximately 85 percent of all serious crimes.

Another perhaps surprising statistic: only about 10 percent of the people arrested are charged with the street crimes which people fear most (murder, rape, armed robbery, forcible assault, and other violent crimes), and even fewer fit the picture that most people have of a criminal. Few people know much about who commits crime, and most people are largely unaware of what happens to a person once he or she has heard the frightening words, "You are under arrest." But almost anyone who is arrested, whether guilty or innocent, develops a keen awareness of our criminal justice system—and the injustices associated with it. A typical apprehended offender may have contact with as many as fifteen persons in the system, including people from the various law enforcement agencies, court systems, and correctional institutions. Actually, there is no one criminal justice system in the United States, where there are at least 60,000 public agencies that in some way deal with criminals. Where city and county agencies overlap, in fact, there is often little cooperation or coordination. So the person who must go through the system may soon change his or her idea of just what criminal justice is in this nation.

WHAT CAUSES CRIME?

What causes crime? This issue has been hotly debated for many years. Theories generally fall into one of two groups. The first blames the individual and stresses biological or psychological factors. The second places the causes of crime mainly on society, or outside the individual.

One of the earliest attempts to prove the internal, or "bad seed," theory was made by Cesare Lombroso, a nineteenth-century Italian surgeon. Lombroso believed that criminals were a kind of genetic throwback to earlier forms of animal life and that they showed special physical characteristics. These included excessively long arms, peculiarities in the eyes, unusual ear and head shapes, and receding chins. A number of outstanding people took this theory seriously. Even in recent years investigators have claimed that criminals were likely to have a muscular body type. They drew a correlation between body type and personality and said that a muscular body type could generally be associated with an aggressive personality.

A more modern "bad seed" theory concerned the famous XYY and XXY chromosome syndrome. In most humans, the X and Y chromosomes are paired so that females have two X chromosomes (XX) and males have one X and one Y (XY). But in some males the cells contain an extra Y chromosome (XYY) or an extra X chromosome (XXY). For a while it was believed that there was a higher-than-average appearance of chromosomal abnormalities in prison groups. Some people went so far as to consider identification of potential criminals by chromosome abnormality as a kind of "biochemistry of sin."

A few times the XYY theory was actually taken to court. In one murder trial, a tall Parisian named Daniel Hugon was the accused. It was reported that Hugon had gone to a hotel on the Place Pigalle with a prostitute named Marie-Louise Olivier one evening in the year 1965. When he was in the bedroom, Hugon discovered Marie-Louise to be much older than he had originally thought. She was, in fact, sixty-two years old. He was revolted by her, declined to go to bed with her, and spent the entire night pacing the floor. In the morning, Marie-Louise awoke and demanded 50 francs. Hugon paid her and then strangled her to death.

A respected geneticist argued in court that Hugon should not be held responsible because he displayed the XYY syndrome. The doctor claimed that people with this syndrome are more likely to be criminally violent; the murder was not really Hugon's fault. The court did not agree. Hugon was found guilty and given a sentence of seven years in prison.

To date, no scientific evidence has proven that men with XYY or XXY chromosomes are unusually aggressive,[1] although in the past, at least one person has suggested that chromosomal makeup be included as part of a criminal's personality file, which already includes blood type.

---

1. Herman A. Witkin et al, "Criminality in XYY and XXY Men," *Science,* August 13, 1976, pp. 547–554.

Although many well-intentioned people think that labeling people in such a way will help to prevent crime, there is at least one good reason not to do it. Tests have shown conclusively that labeling a person as a criminal may encourage that person's criminality.

Although Richard Speck wore a label tatooed on his arm, "Born to raise Hell," it appeared to be more than a label that contributed to the famous crime in which he massacred eight women.

Very early on the morning of July 14, 1966, Speck herded four student nurses into the rear bedroom of their dormitory and stabbed them to death, after promising not to hurt them. He then strangled four others. One student nurse escaped death by hiding under a bed, where she was believed to have been forgotten by Speck. Richard Speck was known to be rough with women, especially after he had been drinking, but the heinous crime for which he was sentenced to 400 years in prison was not caused by the effects of alcohol alone. A psychiatrist who thoroughly examined Speck expressed the opinion that he was a killer because of brain damage. The lethal outburst was believed to have come from head injuries that caused the brain damage.

The part which head injury plays in criminal behavior is a subject of some controversy. A high incidence of head injuries has been noted in case histories of prisoners, but the question has been asked whether the head injury was a causative factor in their criminality or whether they are people who are generally accident prone. Certainly, most brain-damaged people are not criminals.

During the early part of the twentieth century, great stress was placed upon heredity and biological disturbances in relation to criminality. Some states even passed laws ordering the sterilization of certain classes of criminals such as sex offenders or those repeatedly convicted of serious crimes. Then the pendulum swung to an almost total disregard for heredity, and the emphasis was placed on criminality as a result of psychological or social factors.

Is the criminal emotionally sick? Are unconscious conflicts responsible for criminal conduct? Various psychological schools believe this is so. For example, according to the distinguished American psychiatrist Seymour Halleck, a person who feels helpless and hopeless may commit a criminal act in an effort to feel in charge of a situation and to experience control, or power. According to Dr. Halleck, crime may be an alternative to mental illness. The criminal is a person who deals with internal tensions through action. When one is engaged in planning and executing a criminal act, the feeling of being pushed around, controlled, or dominated by others decreases.

Some crimes appear to be committed in an effort to relieve a feeling of guilt. Certainly, in such cases, fear of punishment is not a deterrent. Many people even confess to crimes they have not committed. Psychiatrists believe these people may be guilty of some minor crime and feel the need to be punished.

Psychopaths are people who appear to feel no guilt. Since they have no inhibitions, their impulses spill over into action. Any prison population will contain some psychopaths. Although the term has been considered a catch-all for many types of psychological disorders, there are some characteristics which appear to be common to this type of person. For example, psychopaths are often very bright, superficially ingratiating, and attractive. They are manipulators who consider other persons as objects to be used in attaining their own immediate goals. Distant goals are sacrificed for immediate pleasure. Psychopaths are said to possess no loyalties and, characteristically, they cannot establish meaningful relationships. Since they do not learn from experience, punishment has no effect. Their antisocial behavior often leads many of them to forgery, swindling, or confidence games. Many are in and out of jail much of their lives.

Rather than considering it an alternative to mental illness, as Dr. Halleck does, crime is often thought to be a symptom of an emotional disorder that involves thrill-seeking as a way to break out of frustration or passivity. Reading or watching crime stories is exciting enough for most people. But for the criminal, action is often a must. Crime may be a game that is played for high stakes in which risks that are not always fully understood add to the excitement.

Consider the case of some high school seniors who were cruising in their cars on a typical Friday night, looking for something to do. They drove around looking for girls, but none seemed interested in joining them. One boy picked up the microphone on the CB radio.

"Breaker one nine" he said. "What's happening on Willow Street?"

"Just the usual," came an answer from another driver.

The friends then drove over to the Willow Street parking lot. Not much was happening there. They sat in the car for a while drinking their usual Friday night beer. Then they drove to an area near the shopping center where a group of cars had gathered. The boys got out and stood around in little groups, drinking beer and listening to their tape decks. Dick, who had been drinking too much, got into a fight with Tim. Things got rough. A broken bottle was picked up and used to stab Tim. Tim bled to death in front of his friends.

Many of the group called to testify at the trial expressed the boredom they felt on weekends. The fight was exciting, but things had gotten out of hand. No one had ever thought of Dick as a typical criminal, but he was full of hostility. This time his lack of control brought him a sentence of second degree murder.

Hostility of men toward women may be expressed in rape. The rapist is believed to be committing violence against women in an attempt to bolster his identity as a man. He may take this way of trying to relieve unconscious doubts about personal courage or sexual adequacy.

The true cause of a crime, even when it is apparently the result of some emotional problem, may be very difficult to recognize. Many times a violent act is committed against someone other than the person who has caused the disturbed feelings. Consider the case of Mr. Wilson, who got into his car, drove over his neighbors' lawn, and swerved back into the street, where he sideswiped another car and injured its driver. Mr. Wilson later admitted that he had been arguing with his wife just before he left the house. He was angry with her, but he had acted violently toward others.

The victims of crime are often acquainted with the offenders and, in some cases, play a part in their own victimization. Consider the case of a wife taunting her husband—who is pointing a gun at her—by saying, "You won't kill me. You aren't man enough to do it." According to reports, in one out of four cases of murder, the victim was the first to resort to violence during the confrontation.

Another cause of crime, as seen by psychologists, is the impulse to retaliate for real or fancied wrongs. For example, the shoplifter who takes something he or she does not need may feel this is a way to punish the store for its high prices. In one actual case, a young man who was refused admission to a seminary set fire to a cathedral in a twisted impulse for revenge.

The causes of crime that sociologists stress are those outside the individual. Poverty causes crowding in cities, exposure to criminals as role models, family instability, inferior educational situations, and other problems that interfere with healthy physical and emotional maturity.

Chronic depression is common in poor neighborhoods,

and no one knows whether it causes poverty or poverty causes it. This emotional illness may be responsible for the behavior of millions of people who are blamed for being lazy, stupid, or content to live as they do. People who are able to mobilize themselves move in one of two directions. Either they rise above their condition through education and/or hard work to become politicians, professionals, and so on, or they take up a life of crime, hoping to get rich and not get caught.

A child who is paid a great deal of money by a drug dealer for running errands may have a difficult time finding the praise of a teacher rewarding. Social pressures from peer groups contribute to many different kinds of crimes. A child who grows up in a community where car theft is a common occurrence is more likely to consider crime a part of normal life than is the child who grows up in an environment where there is less visible crime.

Various studies have attempted to explain why more blacks than whites are arrested for violent crimes. As far back as 1967, the President's Commission on Law Enforcement and the Administration of Justice concluded: "The Commission is of the view that if conditions of equal opportunity prevailed, the large differences now found between Negro and white arrest rates would disappear."

In 1971, the Task Force on Individual Crimes of Violence included the following in its report to the National Commission on the Causes and Prevention of Violence: "To be young, poor, male, and Negro, to want what open society claims is available but mostly to others, to see illegitimate and often violent methods of obtaining material success, and to observe others using these means successfully and often with impunity—is to be burdened with an enormous set of influences that pull many toward crime and delinquency."

More recently, Charles E. Silberman, in his highly acclaimed book, *Criminal Violence, Criminal Justice,* suggested that the new awareness of black power owing to a release from older cultural controls helps to explain why blacks commit a disproportionate number of the nation's violent crimes. He feels that blacks sense the white people's fear and that, after 350 years of oppression and fear of whites, this is an extraordinarily liberating force. Where handguns and hard drugs proliferate, young blacks find it easy to "strike out." And while they are striking out at whites, they frequently commit crimes against other blacks who happen to be around.

There are honest and dishonest people in poor as well as in affluent communities. There are criminals who have grown up in law-abiding homes at all levels of society. However, role models seem to be a major factor in the cause of crime in any class of people. Any exposure to white collar crime may increase such behavior. Income tax evasion, political corruption, and other kinds of fraud are forms of lawbreaking that are less feared than burglary and assault. Not all kinds of crime meet with the same amount of condemnation. But living in an environment where lawbreaking of any type is accepted tends to encourage criminal action in others.

In any environment there is interaction between the person and his or her surroundings. If exposure to a criminal pattern is strong, the person is more likely to become a criminal. No one knows how much each factor—heredity, community, family environment, biology, or emotional stability—plays in causing crime. Each individual is different and each crime is different. One cannot say that a person is a criminal only because of conditions from without. Each factor has its influence and the mix may be too complex to determine.

One popular theory on criminal behavior suggests that it comes about as a series of events, with each event contributing to the cause. It may well be difficult to determine, for example, whether the child of an alcoholic father became a delinquent because of the father's behavior or whether the father drinks too much because the child has emotional problems. Does a child become a psychopath because its mother rejects it, or does the mother reject the child because of the child's personality?

The present state of our knowledge is such that no one can tell exactly what causes crime, but this does not mean that the search should not go on. Obviously, removing some of the factors which lead to crime is an important part of prevention.

CRY HELP!

How many crimes are committed a year? No one will ever know for sure, since there are so many cases in which people are afraid to cry for help or in which they feel that it would do no good. Consider the following example, which really happened.

Susan lived alone in an apartment. One Tuesday, she noticed that several packages delivered to her had been opened and rewrapped. Nothing was missing. At this time she was also receiving some disturbing telephone calls. Each time the caller was a man who asked for another man, then said he had dialed the wrong number and hung up.

On Friday of that week Mr. Simon, who lived next door, came by to see Susan. Susan had never met Mr. Simon socially, but she had seen him in the building. He asked if he might come inside to talk with her.

After Mr. Simon got into the apartment, his manner changed completely. He accused Susan of hiding a man there. Susan denied this, wondering what business it was of his. Then she noticed a gun in her neighbor's pocket. Mr. Simon accused the "man" in Susan's apartment of playing the stereo too loudly, disturbing Mr. Simon's sleep. Susan apologized, since she might have been guilty of this, and promised to see that he was not annoyed again. After Mr. Simon left, Susan thought about calling the police and asking them to arrest her neighbor for carrying a gun or to protect her in some way. Then she wondered if this would only make her neighbor angrier, so angry that he would harm her in some way. Rather than report the incident, Susan moved to her sister's apartment in another neighborhood.

Had a crime been committed here? Susan had invited the neighbor to come inside her apartment. Perhaps the man worked as a security guard and had a permit to carry a gun. Certainly he was a strange, confused man. Such a man might be dangerous. But Susan felt that a cry for help to the police was not the answer.

The case of Larry was quite different. Larry garaged his car in the basement of his apartment building. He had not used the car for several days, but when he went to drive it one morning he found that it had been damaged. One or more vandals had apparently jumped onto the roof and hood of the car and then had smashed the fenders with a heavy object. The tires were flat also.

Larry called the police, who came to inspect and then made out a report. But they doubted that they could be of any help. The case never went any further in the criminal justice system.

Mrs. Wright went to the store almost every afternoon at about three o'clock. One day she returned home earlier than usual and trapped a burglar in her house. He fled down the hall, ran into the master bedroom, and closed the door. That left him no place to go but through the window. He jumped out, smashing the storm window, ran through the woods behind the house, and disappeared. Mrs. Wright's neighbor was in the garden and saw the man. When the police came to check for fingerprints, the neighbor denied having seen the man. She did not want to become involved. The man was never caught, and the jewelry taken from Mrs. Wright's house was never found.

Two of the three examples given above were reported and became part of police records, but neither was ever solved. Only in the last case did there appear to be any real attempt to solve the case. However, here, as in so many cases, the attempt to solve the crime was blocked because a witness would not cooperate.

Consider the case of one couple, who were visiting a relative in the hospital when thieves broke into their home. Some material possessions were stolen, but what upset the couple most was the way their dog had been butchered and left to die. When the police came, neighbors refused to testify about anything they had seen because they did not want to get involved. Six years later, the same couple's home was burglarized again. Someone in the neighborhood had seen the burglars and told what he knew to the owners but refused to talk to the police. So again there was no witness available, no arrest, and no action beyond the police report. This complicity of silence has been called a license for criminals.

Witnesses are prone to be uncooperative partly in fear of reprisal. But the effectiveness of the criminal justice system depends on witnesses as well as on the police. And, as a study by the Institute for Law and Social Research has indicated, witnesses usually do not feel that they get enough protection.

Fear is not the only reason why witnesses refuse to help. Many people object to the time they may lose from work or personal activities as a result of court appearances. One witness to a supermarket robbery was called back to court forty-six times. Usually, witnesses are much less involved than this.

Finally, many witnesses are afraid that they will be abused, ignored, or verbally attacked when they testify in court.

To help deal with some of these problems, the Vera Institute of Justice has set up a program out of one Brooklyn courthouse. This program provides free transportation to court, day care for children of witnesses, a special hotline for prospective witnesses through which they can find help, and a special reception center for witnesses who are to testify in the court.

A variety of victim-witness assistance programs are in operation throughout the United States. The National District Attorneys Association, for example, has expanded to sixty-eight offices throughout the country in the last few years. Organizations such as the Junior League are playing a helpful role, too. In Chicago, it is estimated that they have been instrumental in reducing by half the number of absent witnesses in one courtroom.

An overall estimate of the number of witnesses who do not appear in court when they are called is hard to obtain. However, the Vera Institute of Justice recently concluded that half of the witnesses in one high crime district of Brooklyn who should come to court do not.

Protection of witnesses is expensive, but the loss of one key witness in a case may mean that case is lost and a criminal set free to commit another crime.

For more efficient functioning of our criminal justice system, education of the public has been called a key. How much do most people know about the workings of the criminal justice system?

In a study *The Public Image of Courts,* prepared for the National Center of State Courts and published in 1978, it was concluded that the general public's knowledge and direct experience with courts is limited. And, unfortunately, those who have the greatest knowledge and experience with courts voice the greatest dissatisfaction. Generally the study showed that people are dissatisfied with the performance of the courts and rank courts lower than many other American institutions, such as hospitals and schools. But, in spite of limited knowledge and dissatisfaction, interest level is high and there is impressive support for reform and improvement of our criminal justice system.

The National Center study also found that the attitudes of the general public are far less simplistic than previous, more limited, studies have indicated. There is considerable difference of opinion, for example, about how to achieve security for persons and property, but the answer "More and better judges" was given by more people than "More prisons" as a way to deal with crime. Finally it was found that there is a profound difference in attitude, with respect to what courts do and should do in society, between the general public and community leaders on one hand and judges and lawyers on the other.[1]

Few acts are more terrifying than assault, mugging, rape, or robbery. Although these are not the most common crimes, they are the ones that create the greatest agony for individuals, both psychologically and socially. Many people are afraid to walk the streets at night. Many city parks are off limits because of crime. Anyone who reads a city newspaper knows of the problems of the elderly, who stay indoors at night and even fear a trip to their local store in the daytime. Rural and suburban crime is increasing too.

But since so many crimes go unreported, no one knows for sure how many crimes are being committed. Although the number of rapes being reported has increased, this crime is still considered to be the one least reported. Suppose a man rapes a girl who is on her way home from school. The girl is walking along a well-traveled street, but the man forces her into his car at gunpoint, drives her to a secluded spot, rapes her, and then returns her to a location not far from where he

---

1. *The Public Image of Courts:* Highlights of a National Survey of the General Public, Judges, Lawyers and Community Leaders, 1978, page ii.

first saw her. The girl is frightened, hurt, and bewildered; she heads for home. Her mother calls their doctor, who suggests a visit to the emergency room of the local hospital. Before she goes, the girl showers and puts on fresh clothes. She is unaware that this will decrease the chances of obtaining evidence. She feels dirty, inside and out, and she wants to wash. At the hospital with her mother, other emergencies are treated first. The man who cut his hand with a chain saw needs immediate attention. The boy who has been hit in the eye with a ball is treated almost immediately. The little girl who swallowed a large number of aspirin tablets must have her stomach emptied. The girl who has been raped waits uncomfortably. When her turn finally comes, the doctor asks her if she encouraged the man, and she finds this insulting. When he examines her, he shows little sympathy. Finally, he suggests that she rest for a while and forget it. The girl decides not to report the rape to the police. Her parents agree that the chances of the rapist being caught are slim and that the daughter has suffered too much already. She will not go through the agony of testifying if the man should be caught. She will live with the problem. "How could justice be done anyhow?" she asks.

In spite of the fact that catching the criminal does often seem hopeless to the victim of a crime, and even though many witnesses try not to get involved, there are many difficult cases in which crimes do get solved. In the case of rape, many hotlines and crisis centers are helping women to face their own responsibilities in seeing that the rapist is brought to trial. New laws are making many rape trials less embarrassing for the victim.

Many times when the crime involves murder, people are more likely to report the evidence that not only starts the wheels of the criminal justice system turning but keeps them turning through the many steps needed to solve the crime. Consider the following true case where a cry for help led to considerable action.

One March afternoon, while a man and a woman were gathering bottles in a roadside dump in a small New Hampshire town, they noticed the partially ice-covered legs of a person sticking out from under a pile of tires. They contacted the police, and within half an hour people were rushing to the scene. The area where the body was found was sealed off, and not even the police were allowed to enter. Since it was determined that the person had been dead for a long while, time was not a factor. Later that afternoon, forensic specialists from the crime lab uncovered the body in such a way that every possible clue would be saved. The assistant attorney general took notes for use when the scene would be re-created in court for the benefit of the jury—providing a suspect was found.

Soon missing person reports and reports of accidental deaths that might account for the presence of the body were being examined. Experts from the crime lab photographed the scene and noted every item that was removed from the frozen corpse. Since the body, which was partially embedded in the ice, was found to be headless and handless, accidental death was quickly eliminated from the picture. After the frozen corpse was carefully chipped out of the ice, it was taken to a funeral home to thaw so that an autopsy could be performed. All of this took place under police guard. The people who had discovered the body made their statements to the police and were told they were no longer needed.

The next morning, a number of other people played their parts in the criminal justice process. Clothing was removed, labeled, and photographed, then placed in individual bags for further examination. The naked body was examined for bruises, photographed, and X-rayed for any clues to identification. The pathologist made a long incision in the chest, examined internal organs, and sent blood and other tissue samples to the lab for further tests.

The date of the murder was placed at late December or early January, based on the repeated freezing and thawing of the body. When the murderer had removed the head and hands, a part of the jaw with a few teeth remained with the body. The teeth could be helpful if there were some other clues as to who the person had been.

Two days after the body was discovered, police released a description of the victim and his clothing through radio and newspapers. Many calls came in, and a list of fifteen possible victims was compiled. This was soon narrowed to three. A woman who came to the lab identified the clothing as her husband's. His dentists recognized their work when the teeth were shown to them.

Now that the identity of the victim was confirmed, the next steps were to determine how the murder took place and to discover who the murderer was. The work of the criminal justice system was just beginning. Many more actors (people who take part in the criminal justice system are frequently referred to as actors) would have to play their roles before this particularly gruesome case could be solved. But here we have seen how even obscure clues can lead to the identification of the body and, eventually perhaps, to the solution of the crime.

Even though the cry for help often seems futile, there are many arrests. And no matter where or why a person is accused, a number of basic procedures will be followed.

FROM APPREHENSION TO TRIAL

What happens to a person who is arrested can vary a great deal. Not everyone travels the same road to justice, nor does everyone find justice at the end of the road. There are many times during criminal proceedings when a person, either innocent or guilty, can get out of the system, or turn off the road.

Police arrests are the subject of much controversy. How an arrest is made can play an important part in whether or not justice is possible. Though the police are mainly concerned with protecting the public from criminals, they must also consider the rights of the accused. The fundamental premise of criminal law in the United States is that a defendant is innocent until proven guilty, and the rights of an accused to "due process" in a criminal proceeding are provided for in the Bill of Rights. Due process are those procedures and safeguards necessary to ensure an individual that he or she will have a fair hearing or trial.

Suppose you are jogging along a beach at night as part of your usual routine. A fire starts in a vacant beach house just as you pass it; you therefore appear to be running away from it. A witness identifies you as having been in the area, and an investigation shows that the fire was a case of arson. You know that you did not light the fire or spill gasoline on the mattress, but you are under suspicion. One of your socks is found in the house. You know you left it there when you used the vacant house for a shower after a swim earlier in the day. Your dog had been playing with your socks, and one was missing when you got dressed. Unfortunately, there is no witness to confirm your presence in the house earlier that day. And even if there were, it is conceivable that you prepared the fire at that time and lit it later.

Under these circumstances can a policeman arrest you, grill you until you are exhausted, lock you in a jail cell, and leave you there until your trial? Well, you could be arrested at least. But there are certain safeguards against the other occurrences. Over the years, the Supreme Court has expanded rulings that benefit the accused. For example, the famous *Miranda* decision laid down some specific guidelines. Almost everyone who watches television has seen a law enforcement officer reading a list of rights to a suspect. The suspect must be informed that he or she has the right to remain silent, that anything said can be used against him or her in a court of law, and that he or she has a right to counsel before and during any interrogation. Then and only then can a legal confession be obtained.

Suppose a young woman accuses a man of assault with a deadly weapon, and the case comes to trial. The man has confessed, but he did so before anyone read him his rights. The confession is then not admissible evidence in the trial. The man is acquitted, even though the prosecutor, the defense attorney, and others know that he is guilty.

The *Miranda* decision appears to work both for and against justice. In some cases, it may make it more difficult to obtain confessions and to prove guilt, and in such cases the scales of justice seem to be tipped in favor of the accused. But by upholding the rights of the criminal the rights of the innocent are also upheld.

A number of surveys have indicated that police have obtained as many confessions after having given *Miranda* warnings as they did before. There is no evidence, in fact, that fewer arrests and convictions are made because of any Supreme Court decision that safeguards the accused except in the case of minor drug offenses. In fact, the evidence seems to show that there are more.[1]

Let us return now to the case of the fire in the beach house. If you were the jogger who happened to be nearby, could the police search your home for possible clues that would identify you as the person who set the fire? The Fourth Amendment to the Constitution prohibits unreasonable searches and seizures and directs that warrants shall be issued only upon probable cause. But the witness and the sock might be considered enough to warrant a search of your house.

Further investigation into the case might reveal that you were overheard saying that you wished someone would burn that beach house. If it were not there, you had often said, you would have a much better view of the ocean from your own home. Also, the beach house is an eyesore. It needs paint and much repair.

A warrant is issued for your arrest with the sock as evidence of your having been in the house. Your nearness to the scene of the crime and your remarks show that you had the opportunity and motivation—reasonable cause—to set the fire. Now you are taken into custody, fingerprinted, and photographed; your possessions are removed from your pockets in return for a receipt. Other pertinent information is recorded while you are being "booked." Once again, you are informed of your right to remain silent, warned that anything you say may be used against you, and reminded of your right to coun-

---

1. Charles E. Silberman, *Criminal Violence, Criminal Justice* (New York: Random House, 1978), p. 201.

sel. Now you are feeling angry and confused. Suppose you cannot prove your innocence. Who is the guilty person? Why is that person free while you are being subjected to such proceedings?

You are allowed to call an attorney, and you may continue to call until you reach one who will take your case. Many lawyers will not accept criminal cases in large cities where the process often involves numerous time-consuming delays, and so you might not find a lawyer quickly. When your attorney arrives, you appear before a magistrate for a preliminary hearing, bail is set, and your attorney provides the necessary funds. He or she arranges with a bail bondsman to pay a percentage of the bail money, and the bail bondsman guarantees to pay the full amount if you should fail to appear in court. Now, you are free to go wherever you wish until you are called for your next appearance.

Not everyone can make bail. In fact, studies have shown that half of the people in American jails are being held there for trial because they cannot provide the money needed to set them free.[2] Bail is the subject of much recent controversy. American justice has been accused of having a double system, one for the rich and one for the poor. One place where this appears evident is in the case of bail. For those who cannot pay for a bail bond, there may be many days, or even months in jail. Although the right to a speedy, public trial by an impartial jury is provided for by the Sixth Amendment, that right is often impossible to guarantee, and many persons who find themselves in jail awaiting trial are held there for a long time.

Experience with releasing individuals on their own recognizance (OR) has been good. If a person is deemed a good risk by a judge, no bail may be required. This often prevents loss of employment and needed income, gives the accused a better

---

2. U.S. Department of Justice, sponsor, *1970 National Jail Census,* p. 1.

opportunity to cooperate in preparing a defense, and allows the accused to avoid the emotional and physical hardship of jail. It may also provide an opportunity for treatment or rehabilitation. Consider the case of the mother who shot her daughter because she thought the girl was better off dead than being a prostitute. This mother was deemed not dangerous to society. Her emotional state was such that she was not likely to go into hiding. Her motive for the killing was protection of her daughter from what she truly believed to be a fate worse than death. The woman in this case was released to a hospital for treatment before her trial.

In many less serious cases, when the accused does not appear dangerous to society, has no previous record, is respected in the community, has good family ties, and so on, release on one's own recognizance is common. Although this practice may help to relieve the terrible crowding in jails to a slight degree, it has been considered to be further discrimination against the poor. Many criminologists believe that the practice of OR consciously or unconsciously influences judges and juries against those who cannot be released in this manner, since it is a reflection on their personal worth or character.

Procedures vary too among the many local systems and sometimes even within one system. If the alleged crime is serious, the accused is entitled to have his or her arrest justified either by a grand jury of peers or by a judge. The purpose of the grand jury is to guarantee that no person be made to stand trial on flimsy charges.

There are two types of grand juries: grand juries that have the power to indict and grand juries whose authority is limited to carrying out investigations. Many of these investigatory grand juries, however, have been described as persecutors rather than protectors, and many states have abolished them at the local level.

The grand jury, too, has been called a weak link in the criminal justice system, perhaps because the secrecy of its workings keeps it out of the public eye. This makes some people suspicious of its fairness. Also, many ordinary citizens who are called for grand jury duty are intimidated by the prosecuting attorney, who represents the authority of the government. The Coalition to End Grand Jury Abuse is supported by many organizations such as the American Civil Liberties Union, the National Lawyers Guild, the American Friends Service Committee, the Association of Trial Lawyers (Criminal Division), and many others.

Even when a grand jury indicts, the validity of that indictment is appealable. The prosecutor appears before the grand jury with witnesses in an effort to show that there is reasonable cause to believe that the defendant committed the felony with which he or she is charged. The defendant may be called by the grand jury during its hearing, but this is unusual. Neither an indictment nor the information presented can be considered evidence of guilt.

Many offenders leave the criminal justice system at this point, either because the grand jury fails to indict or because a judge considers the evidence insufficient to hold them. On some occasions, a miscarriage of justice at this early stage may result in a dismissal. For example, even a person who is charged with the crime of murder might be released on a technicality, such as might occur if the grand jury is not composed of a cross section of the community in which the defendant lives.

After a grand jury indictment or an "information" (a legal document filed by the prosecuting attorney, which has the same effect as a grand jury indictment), the next step is arraignment in trial court. Here the records are confirmed and the defendant is informed of the charges and given the opportunity to enter a plea. For example, if you were still being charged with arson at the beach house, you would stand before the trial court and enter a plea of not guilty. However, if you were guilty, you might enter a plea of *nolo contendere,* which means you will not contest the charge. Or you might enter a plea of guilty. With either of the latter two pleas, you forfeit the right to a jury trial.

Most people who get to this point plead guilty, since all but those who appear clearly guilty have been screened out of the system. The vast majority of criminal cases are disposed of without a jury trial. When a guilty plea is about to be entered, the commonly used but highly controversial procedure known as plea bargaining takes place. This process, in which the charge is reduced in return for a guilty plea, has been the dominant means of settling cases in the United States for the last hundred years, although many people mistakenly believe it is a recent technique used only because of crowded court schedules.

The practice of "copping a plea" is a common one in American courts, where only about ten percent of the cases actually go to trial. In addition to those that end in guilty pleas, many other cases are dismissed for lack of evidence or because of new evidence found during the investigation. It has been estimated that if the number of guilty pleas were reduced from 90 percent to 80 percent owing to a decrease in plea bargaining, the United States would have to double the number of judges, court reporters, jurors, and other actors in this part of the criminal justice system. Courtrooms and other facilities would also be more crowded than they already are. In Manhattan, hundreds of people are arraigned each day in criminal court. If only one percent of these cases were to proceed to full-fledged trials, the system would collapse.

All along the path of the system, there is an effort to get rid of any cases that will not hold up. This makes it possible for many guilty people to go free. Plea bargaining disposes of the largest number of cases in many areas. However, many charges are reduced to lesser offenses even before plea bargaining, during preliminary hearings.

Why is plea bargaining controversial? Most states recognize and condone plea bargaining, as do the American Bar

Association and the Supreme Court. But although plea bargaining is expedient, opponents claim that it lends itself to abuse. Court calendar fixing may require precedence over justice. Many a criminal has turned the overload of cases to his or her advantage. On the other hand, some prosecutors routinely file exaggerated criminal charges in order to gain a bargaining advantage. Critics say that plea bargaining gives criminal law the appearance of commercial negotiation, even comparing it to bargaining in a Moroccan marketplace. Occasionally, plea bargaining may result in a guilty plea from an innocent person who sees it as the easiest and cheapest way out of the system.

However, until fewer cases pour through the criminal justice system, plea bargaining appears to be one of the best ways of coping, especially in the large city criminal courts.

To better understand arraignment procedures, let us take a look at what might happen on any one day in a large city courtroom.

The judge sits on a raised chair behind a long desk. Police officers, prosecutors, public defenders, court stenographers, deputies, and others stand around waiting for the prisoners to be brought in from the crowded lockup. There are more than thirty cases scheduled for this morning. The court seems cluttered with people moving about or just sitting, waiting for other people. A man in uniform, known as the bridgeman, pulls folders from the clerk's table.

Legal red tape consumes the first two hours of the morning. Then the clerk shouts, "Quiet, quiet in the court." The drama begins. The bridgeman calls out a case by its docket number, perhaps a long one since cases are numbered consecutively from the beginning of the year. First is the case of an elderly woman who is pressing charges against a young man. The woman had testified earlier concerning the time she was knocked down and had her pocketbook stolen with most of the money from her welfare check in it. A few days after the incident, she had identified the robber in a lineup at the police station.

Today, the elderly woman is asked if she is certain that the man who was brought from the lockup is the same one who stole her purse. He does not look the same. She is not sure if he really is the same man. The judge dismisses the case. The identification must be positive, and there are no witnesses other than the victim. The young man is set free.

Another case is called. A legal aid lawyer who will handle the defense has had only a short time to review the case. A young woman and her male roommate are accused of having tried to drown the woman's five-year-old child in a bathtub. Evidence against them is strong. The lawyer has persuaded the woman to plead guilty and to testify against the man, in the hope of being given a light sentence. The judge sentences the woman to a maximum of four years and sets the date for the trial of the other defendant.

A steady parade of people, charged with drug offenses, loitering, and disorderly conduct now passes before the arraignment court. A father asks that his son be committed to a rehabilitation program to help him overcome a drug problem. Mothers sob nearby. A young couple asks for a withdrawal of the charges against them. The husband had broken a chair over his wife's back in an argument, and she had slashed his hand with a kitchen knife. Now they want to leave together. The judge grants a withdrawal and wonders if the battered wife will appear before him again, with more serious injuries the next time.

Many cases are not new. Some have been held over for years by manipulations on the part of the defense attorney. The reasons for court delays are numerous. The arresting officer may not show up. Sometimes the defendants fail to show up in court, and sometimes the lawyers are not there to defend or prosecute them. Or, lawyers for the defense or prosecution might claim they are not ready. Medical examinations which have been ordered are not always completed in time to move the court machinery ahead. Untyped transcripts can cause delays. One need seems to prevail, and that is the need for more. It may be more courtrooms, more judges, more lawyers, more typists, or more of some other actor in the system. All this adds up to court delay. In one case, a robbery suspect was freed because the victim could not be found. He had moved the year before the trial, leaving no forwarding address.

The judge sets hearings for many defendants and drops charges for many others. This day, a group of about eight or nine prostitutes are called before the bench. They were picked up and arrested by plainclothes policemen and taken to the holding cell at the criminal courts building. Now they appear before the judge, but because of a technicality the arrest was illegal. The district attorney does not press charges, and so the case is dismissed.

Another known prostitute appears before the judge. In this case, the defendant has been arrested legally and is pleading guilty. The charge is one punishable by less than three months in jail; the judge will hear the plea and set sentence. He fines the woman $250, with a month to pay, or ten days in jail. The prostitute walks out of the courtroom and back to her street corner, where she will earn enough money to pay her fine before the month ends and before she is arrested again on the legal merry-go-round on which she lives.

When the day ends for the people who work in the arraignment court, there are many cases left over. Sometimes night court continues until 2:00 A.M., but even then, some defendants do not get arraigned. They must be taken back to the precinct in which they were arrested, held overnight, and brought back again for arraignment in the morning.

Many courtrooms are in action at once in a large city courthouse. At 100 Centre Street in New York City, there are twenty-one parts of the State Supreme Court where the most serious crimes, such as murder, robbery, and grand larceny, are being considered. At the same time there can be as many as fifteen parts of the criminal court in action, dealing with less serious crimes.

Not all courts are this busy. In rural areas, just one prisoner may be sitting on the bench after his trial awaiting his transfer to the local jail or house of correction. The case has been heard by a magistrate, with the county district attorney arguing for a harsh punishment and ignoring the pleas of the defense attorney for leniency. The prisoner's remorse, his offer to repay what he had stolen, family difficulties, and poor personal health did not help the defendant's lawyer in his attempt to reduce the charge. When the jury returned with the verdict, the district attorney was pleased with the foreman's, "Guilty as charged, your honor."

This district attorney takes pleasure in winning a case. He is an elected official, well liked in his community because he takes a hard line on crime. He is proud that more people have been incarcerated in the state prison from his county than from any other county (on a per capita basis) in his district. It makes him feel that he is doing a good job.

Each of the several thousand district attorneys in the United States has individual feelings about how justice should be served. For most of these prosecutors, the backlog of cases must be taken into account. But in every case, the position of prosecuting attorney is one of power. Prosecutors make important decisions at many stages along the road to justice or injustice. Judges, too, have sweeping powers.

Since most people never come into personal contact with a criminal court, they visualize it as a place where a trial is being held. It should be evident from this chapter that much more takes place there. Much time in criminal court is devoted to relatively undramatic pieces of administrative business. Of the few trials that are actually held, the majority are conducted without a jury.

The fact that there are so many kinds of courts results in

a confused picture, and the fact that each kind of court is customarily a separate unit adds even further to the problem.

Lower courts in the United States are set up on two series, one state and one federal. Federal courts deal with crimes that involve federal property, that are directed against the federal government, or that involve transportation of illegal goods across state lines.

Although the situation varies from state to state, there are usually the following kinds of state courts in each state:

Inferior Courts: police courts, justice of the peace courts, magistrates' courts, recorders' courts, municipal courts
   Functions:
   To render final decisions in minor cases (subject to appeal)
   To hold preliminary hearings in felony cases
   To consider release on bail or on one's own recognizance
Trial Courts: district courts, circuit courts, county courts, superior courts, and quarter-session courts
   Functions:
   To render final decisions in cases which have come from preliminary hearings (subject to appeal)
   To dispose of cases appealed from inferior courts
Specialized Branches of Inferior Courts and Trial Courts:
   Function:
   To deal with types of offenses named by the above specialized courts
Appellate Courts and Supreme Courts:
   Functions:
   To deal with cases on appeal from trial courts
   Original jurisdiction in restricted fields

A case may enter or leave the system at any one of several levels, and a decision reached in one court may be reviewed and reversed by a higher court. The system has been compared to a pyramid, with the court hierarchies of the federal and state courts rising toward the United States Supreme Court, which is at the top of both. The United States Supreme Court is the federal court of last resort and the court of last resort in most kinds of state cases.

You may find yourself in a trial court if you are still maintaining your innocence in the case of arson at the beach house. Here, proceedings seldom resemble those on television programs, but the actors in the courtroom are much the same. Your lawyer has prepared the case to defend you against the accusations of the prosecutor. You have no witnesses to prove that you did not start the fire. The prosecutor can call to the stand the person who saw you in that area, but you can be sure that no one will testify to having seen you commit the crime since you did not do it.

A jury has been chosen to impartially represent the community's standards of justice. It will decide whether or not the state has proven guilt beyond a reasonable doubt on the basis of the facts of the case as argued before them. The judge serves to review the decisions of the prosecution and is, like the jury, an unbiased representative of the community's standards of justice.

Since all the evidence in this case is circumstantial, it is not surprising that you are acquitted. Nevertheless, you have been through a harrowing experience and an expensive one.

Even a trial cannot *always* guarantee justice for an innocent person. No one knows how many people in institutions are there for crimes they did not commit. There are some known cases in which the wrong person has been incarcerated and later found to be innocent.

One of these was the famous case of Freddie Pitts and Wilbert Lee. Both men were charged with the murder of two white gas station attendants in Port Saint Joe, Florida, in 1963. Pitts and Lee were part of a group of blacks who had been arguing with the victims on the evening of the crime. After making "confessions" that appeared to have been coerced, they insisted that they were innocent. It wasn't until twelve years later, after considerable investigation and the confession of another person, that they were released with a full pardon and given $100 each by the state. Without the help of a reporter, Gene Miller of the *Miami Herald,* these men would probably still be serving time as criminals in spite of their innocence. The person who admitted to having committed the crime was already serving time for another murder. This case is described in detail by the reporter in his book, *Invitation to a Lynching* (New York: Doubleday, 1975).

Cases in which people are wrongly accused and later found to be innocent often make the headlines or constitute material for TV shows. But in most cases the innocent are soon weeded out of the system. Many people who are familiar with courtroom trials only through books or television programs may be getting the wrong impressions.

In order to show an actual murder trial to the public, the case of Ronney Albert Zamora was televised in Florida, where cameras are allowed in the courtroom without the permission of witnesses, defendants, or jurors. After being shown for nine nights in the Miami area, the film of the trial was edited and shown nationally on public television. A partial script for this ninety-minute television presentation, known as *TV on Trial,* can be found later in this book.

Because of the seriousness of the crime, Ronney Zamora was tried in adult court even though he was only fifteen years old at the time the crime was committed. Three months before the trial began, Zamora admitted he had shot and killed Elinor Haggart. The eighty-two-year-old widow, who lived next door to Ronney, happened to walk into her house when Ronney and a friend were in the midst of burglarizing it. The boys took $400 and Ronney shot Mrs. Haggart in the stomach with a pistol he had found in the house.

In spite of pleas of "involuntary television intoxication"

(the defense claimed that excessive exposure to television violence had distorted the boy's concept of right and wrong), Ronney Zamora was found guilty of murder in the first degree by the jury. He was sentenced to the State Department of Corrections for the remainder of his natural life, without parole for at least twenty-five years.

The court also recommended that Zamora be placed in a youthful offender facility and be given the benefit of whatever psychiatric care was available.

Zamora's lawyer is one of many who have tried to prove that their clients are "legally insane." What this means, as well as what can be done with a person who is convicted on such a charge, is receiving much attention at the present time.

The trial, which is often considered the high point of the criminal justice system and the symbol of justice, often raises the question of whether or not the defendant knew right from wrong when the crime was committed.

The famous M'Naghten Rule, which originated in England in 1843, has always been the basis for insanity trials in the United States. The original rule asked if the defendant knew the nature and quality of the act and was able to distinguish right from wrong. In 1954 and again in 1962 the rule was modified so as to base the decision on whether or not the defendant had "substantial capacity either to appreciate the criminality of his conduct or to conform his conduct to the requirements of the law." Under this version, which still holds today, a person may be found innocent by reason of insanity if he or she was out of control while acting, even though he or she knew right from wrong. This introduces the concept of "irresistible impulse," something which has almost been impossible to prove or disprove.

Only about three percent of insanity pleas are accepted by juries. And even if a person is acquitted on grounds of "legal" insanity, he or she may be committed to an institution for a term longer than might have been the prison term following a conviction. Finally, on release from the institution, the person may still be tried on the original charge, now that he or she is mentally competent.

In any trial, the case is always the government versus the defendant. Evidence is presented to sway the jury toward the defendant's case or toward the prosecution. After all the evidence has been given, the judge, in a jury trial, gives written instructions to the jury, telling it how the law applies to the facts of the case. Arguments by defense attorney and prosecutor follow, and the jury is then charged to consider the case on its merits and return with a just verdict.

Then the jury is sequestered (isolated) from other people so that it will not be influenced by them, and it deliberates whether or not the defendant is guilty. In some instances, the vote does not need to be unanimous for a conviction. But in most, unless all the jurors agree, the trial will be declared a mistrial on the basis of a divided, or "hung," jury. Then another trial will be held, unless the prosecutor decides otherwise.

Assuming a verdict has been reached, the judge renders the official judgment based on the signed verdict which has been handed in by the foreman or forewoman of the jury. Sentence is imposed by the judge at a somewhat later date. If the defendant has been found guilty, he or she may appeal the conviction. In some cases, appeals continue for a long period of time, and during this time the convicted person may be free to circulate in society.

"GUILTY AS CHARGED!" WHAT NEXT?

A seventeen-year-old girl was given enough barbiturates to kill her and then left to die. The three men deemed responsible for her death received sentences which varied from one to fifteen years. Two had pleaded guilty to voluntary manslaughter, as a result of plea bargaining, and the third received a sentence of one year for having agreed to testify for the state. The girl's mother is extremely bitter toward the offenders, toward the criminal justice system, and toward society in general. She believes that the men should be serving sentences for first degree murder.

Most victims and their families feel that sentences are too light. Many seethe with feelings of hostility. Only occasionally does one find a victim who remarks that five years is a long time in anyone's life, that the offender is sick and should have had treatment when younger, or that the offender got "what was coming." Few think that justice has been served. One man, the father of a rescued kidnap victim, in reaction to hearing that the men responsible for the kidnapping received sentences ranging from twenty-five to forty years, said, "I don't think it was enough punishment for the crime. . . . I just hope we can do enough to frighten bad people. They need to be scared."

Does the threat of a long sentence prevent a criminal from committing more crimes? Many experts think that short, immediate punishment plays a more important part in crime deterrence. There has been considerable study and discussion over how long sentences should be, how to make the punishment fit the crime or the criminal, and the entire role of detention in crime prevention.

These subjects seem especially important in recent years. After a long-standing lack of interest in what happened to a criminal who was apprehended and punished, the public became more aware of crime and punishment in the 1970s. In addition to being fearful for their personal safety, many people came to realize the cost of punishment both in the economic sense (building and maintaining institutions) and in what prisons and jails were or were not accomplishing.

Many studies continued to report that the causes of crime were deeply embedded in the social fabric, but it was also acknowledged that causes of crime would always exist. The Law Enforcement Assistance Administration (LEAA) was established in 1968 and given a large budget for the purpose of preventing crime. Although the money spent on research and invested in the support of existing systems has helped to defray the rising costs of the criminal justice system, many critics feel that the LEAA has not notably advanced toward its objective of preventing crime. Robert McKay, Director of the Justice Program of the Aspen Institute and former Dean of New York University Law School, has said that the LEAA should never have been expected to prevent crime. "We remain sadly deficient in understanding the problems of crime in the United States and even of the system by which we purport to deal with it. Experts on the American criminal justice system do not agree about some of the most basic issues." [1]

---

1. Testimony before the House Subcommittee on Domestic and International Scientific Planning, Analysis and Cooperation, 1978.

Many comments by officials in the criminal justice system are derogatory.

"The criminal justice system as it stands today is inefficient, costly, and mostly ineffective," says a man who has worked in it for many years.

"The system is in a state of crisis," remark many people who have contact with it.

"Nothing really works," say many of the people who work with criminals.

Although the whole area of crime prevention and criminal justice is being explored on many fronts, controversy over what should happen after a conviction is especially intense. Should the convicted criminal be given probation, a fine, a short sentence, a long one, a minimum and maximum sentence with chance of parole? No matter what the crime or what the sentence, some people will think the punishment must be tailored to fit the crime, while others think it must be tailored to fit the criminal.

When a sentence with a minimum and maximum time is given, a parole board decides whether or not the offender has been rehabilitated and is ready to reenter the community. If only a single sentence has been given, the parole system is usually given the power to release a prisoner after a portion of the sentence has been served.

Parole, a method of releasing prisoners prior to the completion of the maximum sentence when certain conditions have been met, was introduced in the 1870s to encourage prisoners to reform and to display a pentitent attitude toward crime. "Good behavior" reduces many sentences and helps with prison discipline.

Suppose a male prisoner is going before the parole board after having served the minimum sentence. He dresses in his best but shabby and out-of-date clothing, things that he wore when he entered many years ago. He is called into the conference room next to the warden's office, where he stands before a long table. The parole board members are seated around the table watching the face of the prisoner. To some he appears wistful; to others he seems sullen or suspicious. His name and number are read, his record is produced, and the members of the board study the abstract of his case, which lies in folders on the table before them. Their case load is heavy, but they examine the record as carefully as time permits. Some members ask questions: Did you learn your lesson? Are you ready to behave? Do you intend to go straight? Do you have a job?

The prisoner may or may not be considered ready for the outside world. The board may send him back for further repentance, or they may consider him ready to be freed. If he is paroled, the ex-convict may find difficulty in making new friends, finding a job, and living in a world that is very different from the one he left many years ago. Many parolees return to their old environments, where they associate with the same people who got them into trouble in the first place. One parolee reports that he was offered at least forty opportunities to commit crime within one month of being released but not one opportunity for honest work. In such situations, many become repeat offenders.

Some ex-convicts find help through groups such as the Fortune Society, a nonprofit organization of ex-convicts and other interested persons. Some parolees manage to make good in spite of the many difficulties they face.

The parole system is the subject of much controversy, partly because of the problems with rehabilitation (some say it does not work; others claim it has never been given enough support) and partly because of the questionable value of a parole board, which has the power to make predictions about an individual's future, though human behavior is generally unpredictable.

Usually, only the bad decisions of a parole board make the headlines. For example, take the case of Charles Yukl. Yukl strangled a girl and mutilated her body in 1966. After pleading guilty to manslaughter, he was sentenced to a minimum of seven and a half years and a maximum of fifteen years in prison. He was released on parole in 1973, but before long he had strangled another girl. He was convicted and sent to prison for this crime, but he will be eligible for parole again in about fifteen years.

Cases such as this make society call for "tough action" on crime, and this may be reflected in cases that are much less serious. For example, Jeffrey, age twenty-seven, may be an example of someone who has suffered unfairly from the current "get tough" attitude. Jeffrey was arrested twelve times while he was growing up, but he later managed to abandon his dependence on drugs and remain out of trouble for seven years. Then he did a foolish thing, which he soon recognized as such. He stole some toilet articles from a supermarket and was caught. He was arrested and sentenced to sixty days on Riker's Island prison for his crime.

Jeffrey's lawyer noted that his short, youthful-looking client would probably have to spend the two months in prison warding off the sexual advances of bigger inmates. He would again be exposed to the prison subculture which had been long behind him. The problem of why he risked so much for so little would be ignored, but new problems would be created. He would lose his apartment, and probably his job, and might become, as a result, a much greater threat to the community than if he had been fined and sentenced to pay back in work the value of the goods he had stolen. The lawyer asks, "Will some innocent person be victimized because a judge decided to be 'tough' on crime?"

Sentences for shoplifting vary greatly, depending somewhat on where a person lives. For example, in Albuquerque, New Mexico, eighty percent of the people who are arrested for shoplifting receive a deferred sentence. If no new charges are brought against a shoplifter in an allotted time, the charge is dismissed. However, in North Carolina, where more people are put in prison in proportion to the general population than in any other state in the United States, the great majority of convicted shoplifters are given prison sentences.

Both liberal and conservative criminologists are concerned about the problem of sentencing. Many judges have reputations for being "too soft." Others are called "hanging judges" because of their harsh sentencing policies. Under most state laws, there is tremendous leeway in the penalties that can be given for a crime.

Consider some examples of what can happen to individuals in the same community under a system that gives judges unchecked, sweeping powers over sentencing. A man is charged with writing a bad check for $200. He is sentenced to nine months in jail. Another man cheats stockholders out of $200 million and makes a personal profit of at least $10 million by the unlawful operation of a chain of nursing homes. He could receive five years in prison, but instead he is sentenced to one year and will become eligible for parole after four months. An eighteen-year-old Puerto Rican boy is sentenced to five years in prison for stealing a car worth $100. A shoplifter who has stolen a $50 bracelet is sent to prison. A businesswoman embezzles $2,000 from her company and receives a suspended sentence with probation. These are just a few examples of what lawyers and others who work in the system refer to as "sentencing disparity."

Many judges are wise, honest, hard-working, and generally free from racial prejudice or political influence, but this is not always the case. A judge may be influenced, consciously or unconsciously, by race, family ties, economic status, appearance of the offender, and so on.

Certainly, there are "soft judges," "hanging judges," and many judges whose sentences are inconsistent. But some judges must work under such heavy case loads that they simply do not have the time to determine what is a fair sentence based on motivation for the crime, background of the criminal, possibility of rehabilitation, and other considerations. If a judge has fifty cases on a day's calendar and he or she manages to dispose of only half of these, one can easily see how little time is allowed for determining justice.

Most sentences conform to what can be expected, but suppose two men convicted of robbery are confined in the same prison cell after they have received their sentences, which are considerably different. It is not impossible that the man with the shorter sentence may have stolen more money than the man with the longer one. This could certainly lead to hostility and aggression on the part of the second man. Many prison officials complain that unevenness in sentencing is a major cause of discipline problems.

"Criminal sentencing today is a national scandal," said Senator Edward M. Kennedy when he led the drive in 1977 and 1978 for a bill that would reform the Federal Criminal Code. This bill, among other things, would have established a commission to formulate rather rigid sentencing guidelines so that criminals convicted of the same offense would receive equal or nearly equal terms, but it did not pass in the 95th Congress.

Sentencing disparity undermines the effectiveness of the entire criminal justice system, said the Twentieth Century Fund Task Force on Criminal Sentencing. However, Charles Silberman, who was a member of this task force, now feels that sentences are not as uneven as they appear, since critics fail to take into account the differences between what sentence a judge gives and what sentence the criminal actually serves.

Since no two cases are alike, many judges take personal pride in their ability to tailor a sentence to the peculiar circumstances of the case. However, one area of mounting criticism over sentencing practices involves the so-called indeterminate sentence. This contains a minimum and maximum amount, so the parole board, not the judge, really determines the length of the sentence. Since parole boards are less concerned than judges with the safety of the public, especially when prisons are overcrowded, they may sometimes unwisely step up release of prisoners or be unfair in other ways.

When "flat time" is substituted for parole, new problems arise. Many criminologists agree that the certainty of punishment may be a better way of deterring crime than the present system, but there is a tremendous problem in determining what would be fair and impartial sentences for the many kinds of crimes. How can mandatory sentences be precise when so many aspects are involved? In one sample code, six years in prison is the recommended sentence for premeditated assault in which serious harm was intended. The sentence would be two years for assault in which serious harm was not intended. Since there may be a difference in the circumstances of each case, how can a criminal's mental state always be fairly determined? There is certainly a narrow border between these two types of cases and the decision as to which is which may mean a difference of four years of a person's freedom.

Another criticism of definite sentencing is that it would increase the relative power of the prosecutor, the person who selects the charge. The parole board and the judge would no longer be able to exercise any discretion. According to Franklin Zimring, "It is unclear whether total disparity will decrease, remain stable, or increase under a regime of determinate sentences." [2]

Sentencing reform is under consideration in most of the United States, and some states, such as California, Indiana, Maine, and Illinois, have recently adopted forms of determinate sentencing. Widespread changes may depend on what happens in the states which have already adopted new laws.

Another area of controversy is the practice of forgiving

---

2. Franklin E. Zimring, "Making the Punishment Fit the Crime" (Hastings-on-Hudson, N.Y., Hastings Center Report No. 6, December 1976), p. 16.

first offenders and getting tough with habitual criminals. While the criminal justice system now operates this way to a great extent, Barbara Boland, a member of the research staff of the Urban Institute of Washington, D.C., believes that the offenders being sent to prison are largely the ones least inclined to commit additional offenses. Most crime is now being committed by young offenders. Actually, the tendency to commit crime seems to peak at age sixteen. Thus a policy which disregards the early convictions for serious crime but demands harsh sentences for later crimes leaves the offender at large during the active period and confines him or her at a time when behavior is improving. Older offenders who have longer records are sentenced to prison more often than younger offenders, even though these older persons may no longer be committing as many crimes.

Barbara Boland does not feel that teen-aged burglars should be given long prison sentences. But she does feel that some significant action should ensue upon conviction of a serious crime, regardless of age or prior record.[3]

Nicholas Scoppetta, former deputy mayor for criminal justice and commissioner of investigation for the city of New York, takes a different stand. He suggests that a concentrated effort should be made to focus the full force of the criminal justice system on the *repeat* offender. He also claims that the net result of sentences that put defendants back on the streets in a short time is "a continual recycling of the criminal population with little or no effect on them or on the crime rate." [4]

Norval Morris and Gordon Hawkins in their book, *Letter to the President on Crime Control,* point out that aging cures all but the most violent offenders. Yet keeping all prison-

---

3. Barbara Boland, "Punishing Habitual Criminals," *Wall Street Journal,* April 11, 1978, p. 24.
4. Nicholas Scoppetta, "Getting Away with Murder: Our Disastrous Court System," *Saturday Review,* June 10, 1978.

ers who have committed violent crimes incarcerated until their fortieth birthdays would result in a different but no less terrible Gulag Archipelago.

Certainly criminality appears to decrease with age, but not everyone agrees at what age. Justice Macklin Fleming says that true crime—which he defines as murder, rape, burglary with bodily injury, child molestation, grand theft, and so on—is most prevalent in the teens and 20s.[5]

Whether short sentences for *everyone* who commits a violent crime, longer sentences for repeaters, or sentences which take the age of the offender into account will help to prevent crime, no one really knows.

The many studies on what should happen to a convicted criminal illustrate a wide variety of approaches to the question, "Guilty as charged!" what next? James Q. Wilson takes a hard line in his famous book, *Thinking About Crime*.[6] He suggests that the criminal justice system be given the function of isolating and punishing rather than rehabilitating. His general position is that crime would be reduced if more people were put in prison rather than on probation. His solution to the street crime problem is to increase the certainty and severity of punishment. Wilson maintains that wicked people do exist and that they should be set apart from others. This would deter crime in more ways than one, since those who are neither wicked nor innocent would be forced to ponder what is done to the wicked and take it as a cue as to what might happen to them should they break the law.

Critics of Wilson's theory cite, among other things, his failure to take into account the tremendous cost of keeping a person in prison. It costs an estimated $13,000 or more a year

---

5. Macklin Fleming, *Of Crimes and Rights* (New York: W.W. Norton, 1978), p. 177.
6. James Q. Wilson, *Thinking About Crime* (New York: Basic Books, 1975).

to house one prisoner. Just one new prison cell can cost from $30,000 to $45,000 to build. Even now, the rising population in prisons is resulting in the use of antiquated facilities, warehouses, and even old warships. Jails, which are locally administered facilities for those awaiting trial or for the serving of short sentences, house many inmates. Jails have been described as the ultimate ghetto, for conditions in many jails are even worse than conditions in prisons, and it is in these jails that those presumed by law to be innocent are housed.

Prison does not appear to reform many criminals, though that is supposed to be one of its main purposes. Repeat offenders account for about eighty percent of the solved crimes in many areas. Authorities believe that, though such criminals may be repeating old habits, they may also have had their criminal tendencies reinforced while they were confined. Certainly, rehabilitation cannot be counted on to reform all prisoners.

Although rehabilitation, or the treatment of the prisoner, has been emphasized, at least in theory, there are other objectives of punishment. One of these is retribution. Society wants to make life unpleasant for the criminal who made it unpleasant for the victim. The famous psychiatrist Karl Menninger, in his book *The Crime of Punishment,* says, "We commit the crime of damning some of our fellow citizens with the label, 'criminal', and having done this, we force them through an experience that is soul-searching and dehumanizing. In this way we exculpate ourselves from the guilt *we* feel and tell ourselves that we do it to 'correct' the 'criminal' and make us all safer from crime. We commit this crime every day that we retain our present stupid, futile, abominable practices against detected offenders." [7]

Dr. Menninger suggests that quick and appropriate pen-

---

7. Karl Menninger, *The Crime of Punishment* (New York: Viking Press, 1968), p. 9.

alties are called for, not a spirit of vengeance. For those who question why so much attention should be given to the welfare of criminals and so little to the victims who have been beaten and robbed, Dr. Menninger points out that those who may become victims are in need of protection more than those who have already been victimized need vengeance. None of us is being protected by "a system that attacks 'criminals' as if they were the embodiment of all evil."

Some judges and other actors in the criminal justice system deplore the retributive urge to punish. The famous jurist Judge Learned Hand once remarked that he did not share the feelings of the public, which demanded that the sinner should suffer. He felt this was a vestige of some very primitive beliefs and emotions.

Judge David Bazelon describes the so-called theory of deterrence by punishment as an intellectual justification of the primitive urge. This does not mean that judges should do away with all punishment. But they can do away with the revenge aspect. Judge Bazelon suggests that one might be encouraged by the fact that the modern urge to punish is more humane than the primitive urge, or seems so. For example in Saudi Arabia, according to some new reforms, the hand of a thief is now removed by an expert surgeon using anesthetic, rather than being chopped off with a hatchet as in the past. An adulteress will no longer be stoned to death, as in biblical times, but will instead be shot. These attitudes, although an improvement over the old ways in Saudi Arabia, are a far cry from what we think of as justice.

For many victims and potential victims, fear has come to replace the desire for revenge. This is especially true for those who watch young murderers being interviewed. More and more reports tell of violent crimes in which a criminal shows no remorse or no feelings at all. In one case, a young man was arrested for the brutal murder of an eighty-year-old woman whom he had robbed of $3.00. When asked by police officers about his feelings afterward, he just continued to eat his tunafish sandwich; from time to time he laughed. In another interview, a young murderer-mugger described how he had killed his victims. He said he never felt guilty after a murder; he usually laughed, since he found killing both droll and mundane. It is not surprising that people, out of fear, want to keep this kind of criminal locked away from society forever.

Many criminologists feel that a spirit of "just deserts" is a proper one in the context of punishment and social control. A man who kills his wife may never be a threat to anyone else, but punishment must affirm minimum standards of behavior. Killing cannot be considered acceptable behavior. In the case mentioned earlier, in which a mother killed her daughter, the sentence was five to fifteen years in prison. Here again, the mother was probably not a threat to anyone else, but given the nature of her crime, prison had to be the punishment.

In some cases, people are sent to prison because there seems to be no other way to deal with them. Everything else has been tried, but they continue to commit crimes. This may have little to do with feelings of revenge, for these people have been given opportunities to make good.

Some of the studies mentioned earlier are concerned with the need to remove the criminal from society for its protection. Much of the discussion about the length of sentences revolves around preventing the criminal from committing additional crimes.

Yet present methods of punishment and reformation have not been noted for their effectiveness in reducing crime rates. Since the percentage of serious crimes that result in arrests is low, and the percentage that result in imprisonment is lower still, the emphasis in prevention must be on the situations that produce crime. Noted criminologists Edwin H. Sutherland and Donald R. Cressey express the opinion that crime is more than the psychological act of an individual; it involves whole networks of social relations. Dealing with these networks is more productive in prevention of crime than is taking individual after individual out of them and permitting them to remain as they were.

Almost everyone agrees that prevention is superior to correction. But while work is being done to change situations that produce criminals, the criminals who have already been produced must be dealt with. So those who are apprehended and found guilty are either released on probation, incarcerated with or without chance of parole, or placed in programs that are alternatives to prison. Probation and parole are the major ways prison population is kept down, but some alternatives are being tried. Work-release programs come in a variety of forms, and some date back many years. In Wisconsin, for example, back in 1914, legislation gave power to local judges to sentence selected offenders to jail but to furlough them during the day to jobs in local businesses. Work-release has been authorized in about two dozen states and is used in the federal corrections system.

Joe, a thirty-year-old man convicted of petty theft, spends his nights in jail in California. Each weekday he rises at 6:00 A.M., showers, dresses in work clothes, eats his breakfast, and leaves the jail to wait on the road for a friend who gives him a ride to work. By 8:00 A.M. Joe is at work operating a forklift for a construction company. Each evening, Joe returns to the jail, checks in at the gate, and returns to his barracks. Joe's job is part of a work-release program that allows him to earn money. He continues to support a wife and child, meet his union dues, pay a small amount to the county for his room and board at the jail, and still have some left over for his personal expenses.

The offenders who participate in work-release programs must meet certain qualifications. Most have been charged with misdemeanors, but certain felons are included in some programs, with each case being carefully considered on an individual basis. Unfortunately, such programs are available for only a small percentage of offenders.

An even smaller percentage of offenders experience "creative" sentencing. A judge may order a person who has stolen to repay the victim. Formal programs of restitution are operating in about twenty-four states, but there is no record of how many people are involved. These programs were initiated for a number of reasons. One is concern for the victim; another is disillusionment with traditional means of treating criminals. And still another is desire to save taxpayers the cost of incarceration.

One innovative judge ordered a marijuana grower to wheel a load of dirt containing one marijuana plant around the courthouse twenty times every Sunday for the next four Sundays. The load was to include a sign reading "Decriminalize Marijuana."

Many people are ordered to repay the victims the money they took from them, usually in small weekly sums. Often these sentences work out very well. For example, a man who broke into a mobile home sales office went to work for the company to pay back what he had stolen. He was hired as a salesman after his debt was paid, and later he became a partner in the company. One forty-year-old burglar who had spent more than half of his life in jail was caught breaking into the home of a minister. Instead of being locked up again, the burglar was ordered to work for the minister. Three years later, he still had no further arrests.

Many offenders are assigned to work in hospitals or for civic, environmental, or other community service groups. While giving the offender a sense of social responsibility, these programs also provide some benefit to the community.

Restitution is an effective correction and rehabilitation tool for many offenders, but authorities counsel against considering it a cure-all for the ills of the criminal justice system. Although it offers an opportunity for a person to pay a debt to society in a personal, tangible way, many offenders do not qualify for this alternative to jail. A large percentage lack job skills or work habits needed to earn a living (a possible cause for their crime in the first place). Violent offenders with long records are seldom, if ever, employable in this kind of program.

Whether a person believes in hard-line punishment or not, jails and prisons are here to stay for a long time. Hundreds of books have been written about the need for better conditions in jails and prisons. One forty-five page report, released late in 1978, describes the deficiencies of the Hillsboro, New Hampshire, County Jail. Among them were:

The lack of training programs for jail personnel, in spite of records indicating otherwise.

The 6 by 8 foot cells, which are 25 percent smaller than required by national health and safety standards.

The lack of day rooms or any recreational or exercise areas in the facility.

The fact that there are no matrons to guard women inmates at night, thereby subjecting many of them to possible "attack, homosexuality, and fellow inmate control."

A lack of inmate grievance and disciplinary procedures.

A lack of on-the-premises medical care and failure to give medical examinations to new prisoners.

If today is an average day, close to 10 million Americans will enter locked cages in the name of justice. They will join 300,000 prison inmates and about 225,000 people awaiting trial or serving short sentences in jails. The lives of most other Americans will continue as usual with little thought to what is happening in the cages or in other parts of the criminal justice system. Perhaps a few will feel safe because so many criminals have been put away. They will not consider the number of offenders who have served only part of their sentences and are again on the streets. Of course, many of these ex-convicts will search for ways to lead the "straight life," and a few will be helped by new programs designed to provide ex-convicts with community-development work. Some will begin to put into action the plans they made in prison for a new life. But at present, the techniques of "straightening out" prisoners rarely work. What happens after people serve time for breaking the law depends mostly on what they are willing to do about it themselves.

LAW AND JUSTICE IN YESTERYEAR

If you had been arrested for a crime long ago, you would have found the justice you received very different from that of today.

In 1584, the assassin of William of Orange was punished for his crime in a hideously cruel manner. The arm with which he had committed his deed was immersed in boiling water. The following day, it was cut off. During the next eighteen days, his flesh was torn with red-hot pincers, he was stretched on a wheel, and he was beaten with a wooden club. Finally, the magistrate in charge, out of pity, ordered him strangled.

As recently as the beginning of the nineteenth century, similar punishments were not unheard of, and atrocities persist even today. A thief in Saudi Arabia may still be punished by having his hand chopped off; however, as mentioned earlier, this action is now performed by a surgeon instead of an executioner with a hatchet.

Horrible and gruesome punishments have been inflicted on offenders in the name of the law throughout history. Although aims and methods have changed, society still considers it necessary to punish those who break its rules.

Further, society has always tried to find ways of controlling people's behavior. In the interest of self-preservation, it has from the earliest times tried to maintain some order in people's relationships and transactions with each other. In primitive societies, custom governed the rules of conduct. Crime was equated with sin, and offenders were punished as expiation, in order to prevent the gods from wreaking vengeance on the entire tribe. For instance, if you had broken some significant taboo, such as committing incest, you might have been condemned to death along with your family so as to remove the source of danger to the rest of the tribe. If you had been guilty of a lesser offense, such as cowardice, you might have suffered public humiliation and then banishment. Actions which affected the society as a whole, such as the breaking of taboos, witchcraft, and treason, were categorized as public crimes and thereby distinguished from private offenses.

Private crimes were those acts considered matters for personal revenge. These included murder, assault, theft, slander, and adultery; they were settled between individuals and families. Even before there were written laws, people recognized that it was necessary to protect personal and property rights. In more structured tribal societies, entire clans had the collective responsibility for avenging wrongs done to individual members by members of another clan. If the offender could not be punished, then vengeance was visited upon the entire clan to which he or she belonged. Any injuries to a member of a foreign clan were not considered criminal by the clan of the perpetrator. No distinctions were made between accidental and premeditated acts; in other words, the intentions of the offender did not influence the manner in which he or she was dealt with.

The carrying out of vengeance was regulated by the ancient code of *lex talionis,* the principle of an eye for an eye and a tooth for a tooth. A murderer might be executed in the same manner he or she had employed in killing, and retaliation was sometimes carried out even against inanimate objects or animals. In ancient Greece, an object that killed a citizen was brought to trial and banished if found guilty. In England, in 1386, a sow was convicted of biting a child; for its crime it was mutilated and then hanged in the marketplace. In 1685, the church bell at La Rochelle in France was whipped, to punish it for having assisted heretics.

Although a desire for exact retaliation persisted for a long time, it was recognized very early that blood feuds were not very satisfactory in one important respect: there was no means of ending them. Thus, the early Germanic and Anglo-Saxon peoples eventually developed a system of compensation that could end blood feuds and retaliations. Under this system, the injured party was offered compensation and was usually forced to accept it. Money paid in compensation was called *bot*. The worth of a man was known as *wer*, the amount depending on his rank and importance. A cow was worth one-and-two-thirds solidii in German money, while the worth of a freeman was 200 solidii. The laws were very detailed and precise in assigning values to all kinds of injuries. For example, an injury as long as the first joint of the forefinger was worth a shilling, and an injury two joints long was worth two shillings. The elders of the tribe or clan acted as an impartial third party in settling disputes. Their decisions were not really binding, though, and their function was more that of peace keeper than judge. Still, this system of justice did represent an advance because it reduced the endless fighting and killing and made the offender at least try to redress any wrongs that had been committed.

Prior to the eighth century, the early penal customs surrounding feud and compensation applied only to freemen and to those who were equal in social standing. Obviously only propertied people were able to make monetary compensation. Corporal and capital punishments were reserved almost exclusively for slaves. However, between the eighth and tenth centuries, punishments such as whipping, mutilation, and death began to be used more frequently for freemen, especially for crimes which were considered typical of slaves, the lower class, or baseborn people. These slave punishments were gradually incorporated into the criminal law as it evolved.

During the tenth, eleventh, and twelfth centuries in England, when the kings became more powerful and were able to extend their authority, the regulation of criminal punishment gradually ceased to be a private matter. Crime was now considered a public matter, an offense against the king, and a breach of public tranquillity. No longer did the victims receive compensation; instead, the king exacted tribute and punishment. The penal system was administered by officers and judges in the name of the crown, and the heavy fines that were levied were a good source of income for the nobility. The principle of compensation for injury reverted to the principle of vengeance. However, the individual no longer had the power; it was now the central authority that took revenge. The penalties for crime became very harsh, partly in order to maintain the authority of the king and partly because of the idea that punishment had a deterrent effect. These developments ushered in an era of great severity and cruelty that persisted for several hundred years. Many offenses that might be considered relatively minor today were punishable by death. In Paris in 1761, a servant was condemned to death for stealing a piece of cloth from her employer. In England, as late as the end of the eighteenth century, there were still more than two hundred crimes that carried the death penalty. Large numbers of men and women went into hiding and lived as outlaws in order to avoid such harsh retribution.

Horrible forms of torture were used, not only in determining guilt but also as punishment for serious crimes. Capital punishment ranged from more or less instantaneous death to the slow, agonizing means of execution reserved for criminals such as the killer of William of Orange, described earlier. The court decided whether the criminal was to die slowly and by what means.

Drawing and quartering was a form of execution in which horses were employed to pull all four limbs from the body. Sometimes, the executioner had to assist in completing the task by hacking the limbs off with a knife. Decapitation, strangulation, and pressing to death under heavy weights were other popular methods of execution. Lesser penalties included flogging, branding with hot irons, chopping off a hand, nose, or lips, cutting out the tongue, public exhibition, banishment, or sentencing to the galleys. Although offenders were sometimes still required to pay compensation or fines, many penalties involved some sort of physical punishment.

Executions and punishments were carried out in public places to set an example, to deter others, and to remind the people of the power of the monarchy. In England, the practice of public executions did not end until 1868. It has been pointed out that these displays did not have the desired effects. In fact, executions often had a carnival atmosphere; people considered them entertainments. As for deterring crime, the crowds of spectators offered ample opportunities for pickpockets and thieves who plied their trade while watching someone being hanged for the very same offense. The condemned person, having nothing to lose at that point, would often make a speech, cursing the king, the laws, and even God. Many people could readily sympathize and identify with the criminal who they would often regard as a hero. In addition, there were many instances recorded in which the crowds rioted and tried, sometimes successfully, to prevent executions which were unusually unjust or cruel. There were so many strict laws and harsh punishments that even the authorities often did not have the heart to enforce them to the fullest extent.

During the Middle Ages and Elizabethan times, many captured outlaws and criminals were sent to work on the galleys. By the end of the sixteenth century, however, sailing ships had replaced galleys and crime was on the increase. What to do with criminals became a problem. England found two ways to solve this problem. Some convicts were sent to work on prison ships, which were generally kept anchored in harbors. The conditions on these ships were horrible, filthy and overcrowded. Many of the prisoners were not criminals but young boys born out of wedlock or abandoned. Others were described as feeble-minded or lunatics. These prison ships were in use for about eighty or ninety years, until 1858.

Many criminals or undesirables were sent to the colonies. By 1775, England was transporting 2,000 criminals a year to America. Conditions varied greatly. According to some accounts, many convicts were cruelly treated; others fared better and were even given land grants after working out their terms. Conditions in the Australian convict colonies were especially horrible, and many prisoners mutilated themselves or even committed suicide in desperation. There are some gruesome accounts of revenge taken by escaped convicts on former camp commanders. One group of outlaws tied an overseer to the nest of a particularly vicious species of ant; when the outlaws returned the following day, nothing was left but the overseer's head and bare bones.

Devil's Island, off French Guiana, was one of the most notorious of the penal colonies. The colonies of French Guiana, in fact, were known collectively as the "dry guillotine," because so many prisoners died there. Decapitation or bloodshed were not necessary because the terrible conditions caused death just as surely as the guillotine. These penal settlements were not entirely abandoned by France until 1945. However, even now, convicts are exiled to live under miserable and cruel conditions in the penal colonies of the Soviet Union, so vividly described by the acclaimed Russian author, Alexander Solzhenitsyn.

Prison as we know it today was not conceived until the nineteenth century, but imprisonment has been used as a means of detention since the beginning of recorded history. In early cuneiform writing, the symbol for prison signified house of darkness. In the eighteenth century, prisons were used primarily as places for detaining accused persons awaiting trial. Very few people were kept in prison indefinitely, and most of those confined were political or religious offenders or debtors. Imprisonment as a punishment in itself had only a very limited place in the system of penalties until the nineteenth century.

Under the influence of reformers in the late eighteenth century, physical punishment, torture, and public executions finally began to disappear. The reformers believed that punishment should no longer be directed at the body, but should "strike the soul," as one French reformer expressed it. Rather than revenge, the object was to reform and to set an example for others. Under the old system of punishment, the body of the condemned was the king's property, on which the king's vengeance could be taken. The philosophy of the new system was that the criminal had offended society and therefore had to make amends to that society. The 1800s saw a gradual transition from corporal punishment to imprisonment, although the early reformers did not envision imprisonment as a punishment in itself. It was too closely associated with the arbitrary use of power by the kings. It was also criticized by some reformers for not being a specific enough punishment; it had no effect on the public, it was useless and expensive, and it maintained idleness and encouraged vice.

Despite all these objections imprisonment became, within a short span of time, one of the most widely used forms of punishment. According to the French writer Michel Foucault, one reason was that the loss of liberty is a punishment that can be applied equally to all in every station of life. He calls it "the penalty par excellence in a society in which liberty is a good that belongs to all in some way. . . ."[1] In addition, the opportunities prison could offer as a means of transforming and re-

---

1. Michel Foucault, *Discipline and Punish: The Birth of the Prison* (New York: Pantheon Books, 1977), p. 232.

training individuals seemed to fit exactly with the philosophy of punishment of the soul rather than of the body.

The Italian jurist and economist, Cesare di Beccaria, was one of the most influential reformers. In an essay written in 1764, he advocated imprisonment instead of the death penalty because death was less of a deterrent. He felt that a long and painful punishment such as penal servitude would make a greater impression. France and Austria, in revising their penal codes at the end of the eighteenth century, substituted imprisonment for the death penalty; criminals were incarcerated and made to work like slaves, often chained together, wearing heavy iron balls around their ankles and living under horrible conditions.

The idea of the penitentiary (literally, a place to repent) was not new but had its beginnings in the workhouses that originated in sixteenth century Europe. These workhouses were used for vagrants and paupers, to segregate them from the rest of society. Michel Foucault cites the Rasphuis of Amsterdam, built in 1596, as the oldest model for the modern-day prison. In the Rasphuis, there was a system of obligatory work, continual supervision, religious readings, and other educational activities, all calculated to make the prisoners turn away from wrongdoing.

In the eighteenth century, a study done in a penitentiary in Belgium concluded that idleness was the cause of most crimes. It was therefore reasoned that the teaching of useful work in prison would reduce idleness and crime.

The English added the concept of isolation to that of work. It was thought that isolation would protect the prisoners from bad influences and would enable them to rediscover the good in themselves, thereby undergoing a spiritual conversion. The first English prison to be established on the basis of these new concepts in penology was commissioned shortly after the United States became independent. Of course, at that time, England had just lost the American colonies as a convenient place for the deportation of unwanted criminals.

Punishment in colonial America did not usually include imprisonment, but consisted of banishment, fining, whipping, or confinement in the stocks or pillory. Because towns were small and their populations fairly stable, strangers were easily identified, and any suspicious or undesirable characters were banished. Thus each town avoided the problem of crime for itself but passed it along for neighboring towns to deal with. The threat of public humiliation was probably an effective deterrent in these small, closely knit communities; people did not want to be placed on display in the pillory and ridiculed by their neighbors. Hanging was a punishment reserved for the most serious offenses and was used as an alternative only when the other methods failed. Jails were only for debtors or for detaining those awaiting trial.

With the growth of large cities, immigration, and shifting populations, communities in the United States changed greatly, and these earlier methods of controlling crime became ineffective. Ideas about punishment were also changing, and imprisonment was becoming a substitute for capital punishment and mutilation in England and the other European countries.

The first penitentiary in the United States was built in Philadelphia in 1790, largely owing to the efforts of the Pennsylvania Quakers, who were leaders in the movement for penal reform. The Pennsylvania prison system was modeled on the English and European systems and was based on the principles of hard labor and solitary confinement. Prisoners were isolated from each other at all times, and they ate and worked in their separate cells. Communication was forbidden. Work was compulsory, and the prisoners were paid. There was constant supervision, and every moment of the day was occupied with some task.

The Pennsylvania system added some innovations, one of the most important being the practice of observing, interviewing, and counseling all the prisoners on a regular basis in order to decide on the best method of rehabilitation and to determine who was suitable for release under supervision. The

Cherry Hill Penitentiary, built in Pennsylvania in the 1820s, carried the idea of isolation to the ultimate degree. It was ingeniously designed, with cell blocks radiating out from a central observation tower, and planned in such a way that the prisoners never saw each other but could be observed constantly. If they left their cells for any reason, they had to wear blindfolds to prevent them from seeing the other prisoners.

A rival system was instituted in Auburn, New York, in 1819, and there was a great deal of controversy over which system was better. At Auburn Prison, inmates were confined to their cells only at night; they worked in the prison shops and ate together during the day. According to those who advocated the Auburn system, its advantage was that it imitated society by having the prisoners associate with each other. Hard labor and strict discipline were the means by which the criminals were to be reformed. Absolute silence was required at all times, and the prison was a silent, grim, gloomy fortress. Cells were tiny, cramped, airless, and dark; none had windows to the outside, for security reasons.

It was at Auburn that the prison lockstep was devised. The prisoners had to walk in single file, right hand on the shoulder of the man ahead, sliding their feet in unison in a kind of shuffling gait and keeping in step at all times. They were also supposed to keep their heads down and their eyes on the ground.

At first, solitary confinement was used as punishment for breaking the rules, but it was found to be too disruptive to prison routine and removed too many prisoners from the labor pool. Physical punishment was therefore instituted. Prisoners were subjected to flogging, stretching on the rack, hanging by their thumbs, and countless other tortures. The punishment of criminals had reverted to the same kinds of punishment that the introduction of the prison was supposed to have eliminated. These methods persisted into the twentieth century.

Most of the prisons built in the United States during the

nineteenth century were modeled on the Auburn system, as they provided cheap labor and were efficient to run. Auburn became the model for the maximum security prison. Of the 133 state maximum security prisons in use in 1973, fully half had been built before 1900. Even into the twentieth century, many prisons were still being built according to the same plan as Auburn.

By the middle of the nineteenth century, it was obvious that the prison system was a failure. Prisons were brutal, inhumane, and overcrowded, and they were clearly failing in their goal of rehabilitating criminals. There were various attempts at reform over the years, but none were very successful. In the early 1900s, there was an effort to normalize the prison environment by abolishing the lockstep, striped uniforms, and the rule of silence, and some effort was made to rehabilitate prisoners.

Before World War II, prisons were very strictly run under an authoritarian system, and the primary concern was to keep peace and order. The prisoners as well as the authorities enforced the system, and the inmates lived according to a strict code that emphasized keeping out of trouble. Although brutality, abuse, and corruption existed, these institutions were fairly peaceful. But the inmates were not rehabilitated and did not learn how to live on the outside; they learned how to "do time." About half of them became involved in crime again after release and were returned to prison.

During the 1950s and 1960s, there was a new reform movement, spurred in part by unrest and riots in the prisons. This movement resulted in a number of new ideas being implemented. Education, vocational training, psychotherapy, and counseling were introduced in varying degrees in order to rehabilitate the prisoners, who were considered "sick" and in need of treatment. The system of indeterminate sentencing was instituted. Terms were to vary from a minimum to a maximum time, depending on the rehabilitation of a prisoner. Parole boards were given the power to decide on the time of release. As mentioned earlier, this method is still being used in spite of controversy about its fairness.

Despite the initial optimism, the new system did not lower the rates of recidivism (return to criminal activity). The prisoners tended to view the system as a hypocritical plan under which administrators did as they wished and disguised it as therapy. In addition, many convicts objected to being labeled as emotionally disturbed. The system of indeterminate sentencing in many cases resulted in longer jail terms than a definite sentence.

During the 1960s and early 1970s, conditions in prisons reflected the rising racial hostilities in the rest of society. While the prison population in former times had been predominantly white, it was now becoming disproportionately black. Ethnic and racial groups were organized within the prisons, and violence erupted between the various factions. Many prison riots have occurred to protest not only the conditions in prison but also the inequality of the system that sends such a high number of minority group members to prison. In 1971, a riot to protest conditions at Attica Prison in New York State left forty-three people dead.

Hostilities and violence are still a problem in prisons. The prison system has failed to deter crime or to rehabilitate criminals. There has been little agreement among experts as to possible solutions, and no acceptable replacements have been found for prisons. According to many criminologists, the history of punishment has been a story of frustration and futility.

YOUR PART IN CRIME PREVENTION

The worst crime may be to ignore crime. Criminal justice professionals emphasize that they alone cannot control crime and that citizen action is an absolute necessity. Various federal commissions that have been established in the last several years to study criminal justice have agreed that private citizens can make a decisive difference in the prevention, detection, and prosecution of crime.

If you ask some friends what they think they can contribute to the crime problem, they may throw up their hands and say it is too big a problem for any individual to consider. Certainly it is true that society has been searching for solutions to crime since the beginning of time. It has been said that no one should logically expect criminologists to provide definitive answers to the crime problem any more than one should expect theologians to come up with an answer to sin. In a review of a three-volume work of 1,600 pages, written and edited by outstanding criminologists, one finds the following: "[The authors] have trained a microscope upon criminals and the institutions that society has created to deal with them, but they have failed to throw much light upon the impact of rising crime on everybody else."[1] No wonder the average person asks, "What can I do about crime and criminal justice?"

Adopting a fortress mentality in which the fear of crime causes withdrawal into a well-protected shell is no solution. Certainly, caution and common sense are advisable for crime prevention, but more action must be taken. Some experts say that the very fear of crime is helping to create the conditions that permit crime to fester.

Although there are no panaceas concerning effective citizen participation in a field as complex as criminal justice, the efforts of many volunteers and concerned citizens in general contribute much to the prevention of crime, the execution of justice in the courts, the improved conditions of prisons, and so on. The old challenge laid down by the President's Commission of Law Enforcement and Administration of Justice in 1965 is even more important today: "Every American can translate his concern about, or fear of, crime, into positive action. Every American should." Today, this applies equally to all of us.

What you do depends on how deeply you want to become involved. Everyone can help to prevent crime by following a few simple procedures in protecting person and property. Many actions are so simple that it is hard to understand why people do not do them automatically. "I was planning to have a better lock put on the back door," is a common remark after a burglary.

Here are some suggestions that can be followed easily but which play a part in crime prevention:

Keep doors locked.

---

1. Review by Fred Graham of *Crime and Justice,* edited by Leon Radzinowicz and Marvin E. Wolfgang. 3 vols. (New York: Basic Books), in *New York Times Book Review,* October 3, 1971.

Make certain that locks are the type that cannot be opened by amateur burglars. Every exterior door should have a quality dead-bolt lock with a one-inch throw.

Secure each window by drilling a hole through the interior frame partially into the exterior frame and inserting a screw that is long enough to reach into the exterior frame. It is not necessarily true that a burglar who wants to get into a house will do so no matter what safeguards you take. Many burglars are on the lookout for houses that are easy to enter. Experts believe that the average burglar will not complete his or her crime if delayed by as little as four minutes.

About three million burglaries are committed in houses and apartments each year in the United States. One occurs about every thirteen seconds, and many of these could have been prevented by deterrence, delay, and detection. Over seventy-five percent of all burglaries require forcing a door or window to gain entry.

Although it is nearly impossible to make a house or apartment impregnable, it is relatively easy and inexpensive to make forced entry difficult and to delay the burglar. You should, for example, see to it that all shrubs in front of your home's doorways and windows are trimmed to remove the cover that burglars value. Lights left on when you are out will also discourage burglary.

Cooperation with community organizations can help to prevent crime in various ways. Operation ID is a program sponsored by many local police departments. By borrowing an instrument from them, you can engrave your social security number or driver's license number on articles that are most likely to be stolen. If you do this, you will have a better chance of identifying any stolen property that is reclaimed by the police.

National Neighborhood Watch is a program designed to help individuals prevent crime. Be a neighbor who reports suspicious signs, such as a person going from house to house in your neighborhood trying door handles. Suspicious cars can often be spotted by people who are familiar with those that belong in a neighborhood. The following actual case helped to solve a number of burglaries and prevent additional theft.

Mr. V(ictim) returned home to find that someone had forced a rear window and stolen his television set. He reported the incident to the police, who came by and made out the usual report but gave him little hope of solving the crime. Children in the neighborhood who noted the police car at Mr. V's house had also seen a strange car parked near a different house. They called the police, who came in time to catch the burglar in the act of removing a television set from a rear entrance. The burglar confessed to a series of similar crimes and was sentenced for the one in which he had been caught.

Participate in Operation Whistle. "Whistlestop" programs encourage everyone to blow a whistle when a crime is observed. When one person hears a whistle, others join in until the police arrive. For example, Mrs. N(eighbor) sees a prowler creeping up a fire escape of the apartment building next to hers. He eases onto the roof and opens a window in the next building. Mrs. N calls the police and blows her whistle loudly, and the burglar scrambles down the fire escape. By the time he reaches the street, other neighbors are blowing whistles and are outside blocking the burglar's escape. In the meantime, a police car arrives in response to Mrs. N's call. Many organizations encourage people to participate in programs by making whistles available at low cost. Whistles are audible proof that fear and frustration are not the only ways to fight crime. Is there such a program in your community?

Report crimes promptly to help police solve them and to help prevent future criminal action. If you are a witness to or the victim of a crime, call the police, identify yourself, and explain as follows:

Give the nature of the crime, the location, the number and

sex of the person(s) involved, whether or not there was a car involved, and, if possible, the license number and make of the car and which way it went. While waiting for the police to arrive, jot down all the information you can remember while the experience is still fresh in your mind. If you saw the suspect, include as much of the following as possible: age, skin color, hair color, size in comparison to your own, clothing (color and condition), speech (accent or peculiarities), marks (scars, acne, tatoos). Write down how the crime happened. Was there a weapon? If so, what kind? Which hand held it? Was a mask or other face covering worn?

The Women's Crusade Against Crime in St. Louis, Missouri, is a particularly effective crime-fighting community organization. Beginning in January 1970, the Crusade was organized to help pass an anti-crime bond issue. After achieving its original purpose, the group continued to work and grow in many directions. It now comprises several thousand volunteers banded together for the purposes of educating themselves and the public on all facets of the criminal justice system, taking action to achieve needed reforms, and teaching women how to protect themselves, their families, and their neighborhoods from criminal abuse. Primarily, the Crusade focuses on problems, possible solutions, and projects in the four major areas of the criminal justice system: police, courts, corrections, and youth.

Whistlestop and Operation ID, mentioned earlier, are two parts of the general program of the St. Louis Women's Crusade Against Crime, but only two. Other parts include a system of allowing witnesses to supply information secretly, jail visits, tours of correction centers, and court watching.

Court watching is an especially interesting part of the Crusade. After participating in an orientation program, men and women, eighteen to eighty years of age, observe and report court activities. Court-related news stories and trends are reported in a court watchers' newsletter, which is published monthly. The purpose is to make constructive recommendations for speeding up trial procedures and improving the dispensation of justice. A staff member (paid by federal grant money) coordinates the activities of the court watchers and answers questions from citizens in the Municipal Courts building. Questions average about three hundred a day.

The St. Louis Women's Crusade Against Crime is a broad program of action. The Crusade was initially a local effort, but it spread to other neighborhoods. Then a two-year grant from the Law Enforcement Assistance Administration was awarded to the Crusade to help members implement their crime prevention programs throughout the United States. If you are interested in more information about this organization, write to them at 1221 Locust Street, St. Louis, Missouri 63103.

One effort in crime prevention, which is part of the St. Louis program, and which is popular in many other communities as well, is the teaching of volunteers to report crimes after training sessions with the police. These people are known as crime blockers. Crime check, crime alert, crime stop, and citizen alert are other names for campaigns to create closer contact between police and citizens. Civilian patrols that serve as eyes and ears for the police are encouraged and, in many communities, police help to train them. Efforts are made to prevent vigilantism. (Vigilantes are people who act as self-appointed guardians of the public and often use violence or threats of violence to cow supposed lawbreakers into submission.)

A model program of community involvement is the Community Crime Prevention Program, which has been operating in Seattle, Washington. This program includes a residential security inspection, property marking, block watches, and the dissemination of information to the public. None of these tactics is original. The difference between this program and many others is the careful coordination, commitment, and cooperation of the police plus the cultivation of a sense of a community in the city's neighborhoods. Evaluation of the program showed that it had achieved its goal of mobilizing citizen concern over the rapidly rising residential burglary rate and of turning that concern into citizen action.

Even if you do not want or cannot afford to spend much time in an effort to prevent crime and improve justice, there are ways in which you can help.

Check to see if your Governor's Commission on Administration of Justice or the Justice Planning Commission in your state wants citizens suggestions on achieving a more effective criminal justice system. For example, in Vermont, the Governor's Commission asks citizens to give their perceptions or opinions on many issues such as the following:

Removing "victimless crimes" from the criminal justice system (e.g., intoxication, gambling, prostitution, homosexuality, possession of marijuana).

Improving arraignment and prosecution procedures.

Taking action to reduce job discrimination practices against ex-offenders who have completed their sentences by
1. eliminating such questions as "Have you ever committed a felony?" on application forms,
2. restricting vocational licensing boards from discriminatory practices, and
3. abolishing those rules which exclude ex-felons for life from certain vocations such as the armed forces.

Improving sentencing by such methods as restricting the use of indeterminate sentences, suspended sentences, and probation; changing parole eligibility requirements; using mandated sentences (flat sentences); making greater use of partial or complete restitution to victims as part of sentence.

Improving crime investigation and detection by overcoming failure to report crimes and delays in reporting; encouraging witnesses to testify against acquaintances or neighbors; improving attitudes toward police and their methods.

You might want to take a stand on a subject that is controversial nationwide and one in which citizen cooperation is especially important. This is the subject of handguns. Surveys taken over the past forty years show that a substantial majority of the American people want some kind of federal control established over the sale and ownership of handguns. Present gun control laws are loose and impossible to enforce. For example, where gun sales are restricted locally, people can obtain guns in a nearby territory where the market is wide open.

Many law-abiding citizens buy handguns in the hope of protecting their homes, but reports indicate that a gun kept in the house for self-protection is far more likely to cause serious injury or death to family and friends than to an intruder. Children and young adults are most vulnerable to firearms misuse. A burglar is more likely to steal a weapon intended for home defense than to be repelled by it. One study done in Chicago indicates that robbery victims who make some attempt at resistance are eight times more likely to be killed than those who put up no defense.

In the case of rape, most victims are taken by surprise. So it is extremely unlikely that the use of handguns will significantly deter rapists. A former police commissioner, Robert DiGrazia, has said that the handgun is useful for self-defense only if you always keep it loaded and are "willing to answer every knock on the door with your finger on the trigger." Experts in the field of violence suggest that though the finger may pull the trigger of the gun, the gun may also trigger the finger. An estimated 100,000 handguns are stolen from law-abiding citizens each year, and these enter the criminal underworld and are used to perpetrate further acts of crime and violence. A loaded gun in the possession of someone emotionally troubled has been compared to a time bomb ready to go off.

According to Handgun Control, Inc. (formerly the National Council to Control Handguns), a new handgun is sold every thirteen seconds, and one American is murdered every hour of every day. Handguns account for about three times as many murders as knives, the next most frequently used weapon in homicides. Without handguns available, far fewer crimes would end in injury or murder.

Most people who favor handgun control are not concerned about rifles and shotguns, since generally these are used legitimately by the estimated 20 million hunters and sportsmen in the United States. Gun control groups are more concerned with the so-called "Saturday night special," a name applied to a variety of inexpensive handguns. Sometimes known as the "ghetto gun," this kind of handgun may kill ten times as many blacks as whites.

Might gun owners be made to register and license their guns, much as they do their automobiles? Might they be required to pass proficiency tests in the handling of guns? Such instruction might, at least, prevent some of the thousands of accidents which occur annually while people are cleaning, loading, or playing with their guns.

If you are interested in doing something about the handgun problem, contact Handgun Control, Inc., 810 18th Street, N.W., Washington, D.C. 20006 and the National Rifle Association, 1600 Rhode Island Avenue, N.W., Washington, D.C. 20036, two organizations which have opposing views. The National Coalition to Ban Handguns, 100 Maryland Avenue, N.E., Washington, D.C. 20002, is another organization which can supply information. Then, after studying the problem, you can write to those who represent you in Congress. Citizens' voices, like citizens' votes, do count.

Opportunities to help prevent crime and improve justice are numerous and varied. *Skills for Impact: Voluntary Action in Criminal Justice,* by Benjamin Broox McIntyre, is a detailed report that cites a variety of approaches for groups that are seriously concerned about street crime and justice. This and other sources of helpful information are listed at the end of this book.

The National Criminal Justice Reference Service (NCJRS) is a national and international clearinghouse of practical and theoretical information about criminal justice and law enforcement. If you are interested in further information about a special subject, you can obtain publications on that subject by writing to NCJRS Document Order, Box 6000, Rockville, Maryland 20850, with the document title and number. Below is a partial listing of those that are available.

Arson Burns Us All	NCJ 44781
Basic Sources in Criminal Justice	NCJ 49417
Careers in Law Enforcement	NCJ 42765
Community Crime Prevention	NCJ 43628
Court Reporting	NCJ 36026
Crimes Against the Elderly	NCJ 43626
Criminal Justice Evaluation	NCJ 25659
Halfway House	NCJ 46851
International Criminology and Criminal Justice	NCJ 39235
Issues in Sentencing	NCJ 47100
Jury Reform	NCJ 48232
Juvenile Diversion	NCJ 34456
	and NCJ 40050
Overcrowding in Correctional Institutions	NCJ 45869
Plea Bargaining	NCJ 32329
Police Crisis Intervention	NCJ 48005
Prosecutorial Discretion:	
The Decision to Charge	NCJ 30983
Public Defender Program	NCJ 49096
Recidivism	NCJ 34360
Terrorism	NCJ 34048
	and NCJ 39646
	and NCJ 45005
Victim Compensation and Offender Restitution	NCJ 32009
Victimless Crime	NCJ 43630
Victim/Witness Assistance	NCJ 49698
White Collar Crime	NCJ 42502
Work Release	NCJ 35886

SUGGESTED READING

Abrahamsen, David. *The Murdering Mind.* New York: Harper & Row, 1973.
Bard, Morton, and Dawn Sangray. *The Crime Victim's Book.* New York: 1979.
Barracato, John, with Peter Michelmore. *Arson.* New York: W. W. Norton, 1976.
Blassingame, Wyatt. *Science Catches the Criminal.* New York: Dodd, Mead, 1975.
Blumberg, Abraham S. *Criminal Justice.* New York: New Viewpoints, 1979.
Carlson, Rick J. *The Dilemma of Corrections.* Lexington, Mass.: D. C. Heath, 1975.
Chamber of Commerce of the United States. *Marshalling Citizen Power Against Crime.* Washington, D.C.: Chamber of Commerce of the U.S., 1970.
Chappell, Duncan, and John Monahan. *Violence and Criminal Justice.* Lexington, Mass.: D. C. Heath, 1975.
Clark, Leroy D. *The Grand Jury: The Use and Abuse of Political Power.* New York: Quadrangle Books, 1977.
Clark, Ramsey. *Crime in America.* New York: Simon & Schuster, 1970.

DeWolf, Harold. *What Americans Should Do about Crime.* New York: Harper & Row, 1976.
Dolan, Edward F., Jr. *Gun Control.* New York: Franklin Watts, 1978.
Fleming, Macklin. *Of Crime and Rights.* New York: W. W. Norton, 1978.
Forte, David. *The Supreme Court.* New York: Franklin Watts, 1979.
Gelb, Barbara. *On the Track of Murder.* New York: William Morrow, 1975.
Godwin, John. *Murder USA: The Ways We Kill Each Other.* New York: Ballantine Books, 1978.
Goldman, Sheldon, and Austin Sarat. *American Court Systems: Readings in Judicial Process and Behavior.* San Francisco: Freeman, 1978.
Greenwood, Peter et al. *The Criminal Investigation Process.* Lexington, Mass.: D. C. Heath, 1977.
Harmon, A. J. *Remodeling for Security.* New York: McGraw-Hill, 1978.
Hyde, Margaret O. *Juvenile Justice and Injustice.* New York: Franklin Watts, 1977.
Hyde, Margaret O. *Speak Out on Rape.* New York: McGraw-Hill, 1976.
Kwartler, Richard. *Behind Bars: Prisons in America.* New York: Vintage Books, 1977.
Lawson, Don. *The Changing Face of the Constitution.* New York: Franklin Watts, 1979.
Loeb, Robert H., Jr. *Crime and Capital Punishment.* New York: Franklin Watts, 1978.
Loeb, Robert, and John P. Maloney. *Your Legal Rights as a Minor.* Rev. ed. New York: Franklin Watts, 1978.
McIntyre, Benjamin Broox. *Skills for Impact: Voluntary Action in Criminal Justice.* The Association of Junior Leagues. Athens, Ga.: Institute of Government, University of Georgia, 1977.

Menninger, Karl. *The Crime of Punishment.* New York: Viking Press, 1968.
Mitford, Jessica. *Kind and Unusual Punishment.* New York: Alfred Knopf, 1973.
Silberman, Charles E. *Criminal Violence, Criminal Justice.* New York: Random House, 1978.
Skolnick, Jerome H., Martin Frost, and Jane L. Scheiber. *Crime and Justice in America: A Course by Newspaper Reader.* Del Mar, Calif.: Publishers, Inc., 1977.
Toch, Hans. *Police, Prisons, and the Problem of Violence.* Rockville, Md.: National Institute of Mental Health Center for Studies of Crime and Delinquency, 1977.
Wolfgang, Marvin, ed. *Studies in Homicide.* New York: Harper & Row, 1967.
Van der Haag, Ernest. *Punishing Criminals.* New York: Basic Books, 1975.
Von Hirsch, Andrew. *Doing Justice.* New York: Hill and Wang, 1976.
Ward, Richard H. *Introduction to Criminal Investigation.* Reading, Mass.: Addison-Wesley, 1975.
Waters, John F. *Crime Labs: The Science of Forensic Medicine.* New York: Franklin Watts, 1979.
Wilson, James O. *Thinking about Crime.* New York: Basic Books, 1975.
Yochelson, Samuel, and Stanton E. Samenow. *The Criminal Personality,* Vol. I, II. New York: Jason Aronson, 1976, 1977.

TV ON TRIAL
The Trial of
Ronney Zamora

Program Host
RICHARD REEVES
National Editor, *Esquire* Magazine

Presiding Judge
THE HON. H. PAUL BAKER
11th Judicial Circuit, State of Florida

The Prosecution
THOMAS HEADLEY
Assistant State Attorney, State of Florida
and
RICHARD KATZ
Assistant State Attorney, State of Florida

The Defense
ELLIS RUBIN
Attorney for the Defense

Guest Commentary
DR. GEORGE GERBNER
Professor of Communication
University of Pennsylvania

Executive Producer
SHEP MORGAN

Producer
DONALD FOUSER

Associate Producer
KARIN DORSETT

TV ON TRIAL was made possible by a grant from the Corporation for Public Broadcasting

A Female Newscaster: . . . search is underway for a car belonging to an eighty-three-year-old woman who was found murdered in her Miami Beach home yesterday. Police say Elinor Haggart was shot to death.
A Male Newscaster: Miami Beach police have arrested two juveniles age fifteen and sixteen in the shooting death of eighty-three-year-old Elinor Haggart.

Richard Reeves: (host) This is courtroom 4–1 in the Hall of Justice in Dade County, Florida. We're going to show you a murder trial that began in here on September 26th, 1977. The reason we can do that is that the trial was televised. It was shown for nine nights in the Miami area. Florida is one of the six states that allow television cameras in its courtrooms. Under a one-year experimental program, it's the only state that allows cameras in without the permission of defendants, witnesses, or jurors. The defendant's name in this case is Ronney Albert Zamora. He was fifteen years old at the time of the crime. Three months before this trial began, he admitted that he shot to death the woman who lived next door to his family in Miami Beach. Her name was Elinor Haggart; she was eighty-three years old, a widow. She happened to walk into her house and she caught young Zamora and a friend named Darrell Agrella in the middle of a burglary. They took four hundred dollars and Zamora shot her in the stomach with a pistol he found in the house.

You'll see Zamora plead not guilty. The reason, his attorney will say, is that the young man was legally insane. He'll try to prove that Ronney Zamora couldn't tell right from wrong. He'll say the boy acted under the influence of excessive television watching. Zamora, the defense is going to say, was a victim of television violence.

There was a television camera in this courtroom. One camera recorded forty-two hours of the trial. Two to three hours of videotaped testimony and arguments were shown each night on Miami's public television station. Local commercial stations selected and edited portions for their nightly newscasts. The hour and a half of tape that you'll see here has been edited—heavily edited. We made more than a thousand edits. A few witnesses will be shown out of sequence because that's the way their testimony seemed to make sense.

A couple of other points before we begin: you're going to see and hear arguments that the jury didn't. When the judge ordered the jury to leave the courtroom, the camera and the microphone stayed. There was also a change of courtrooms during the trial, so sometimes the jury and witnesses will appear to have changed sides of the room.

The Court is called to order. The judge is the Honorable Paul Baker; the defense attorney is Ellis Rubin; and first we hear from the prosecutor, Assistant State Attorney Thomas Headley:

Judge Baker: Mr. Headley, you may begin your opening statement.

Mr. Headley: May it please the Court, Mr. Rubin. Good morning, ladies and gentlemen.

This is my opportunity to make to you what is known as an opening statement. The purpose of an opening statement is to give you an outline of what I expect to show in the State's case. We give you a skeleton of the entire case at this point, so you will better understand the bits and pieces of testimony as it comes from each witness on the witness stand. I will take this opportunity to read to you the indictment.

State of Florida Versus Ronney Albert Zamora

In the name and by the authority of the State of Florida, the grand jurors of the State of Florida present that between the third day of June, 1977, and the ninth day of June, 1977, within the County of Dade, State of Florida, Ronney Albert Zamora unlawfully and from a premeditated design, in an attempt to perpetrate a burglary, did kill and murder the said Elinor Haggart, a human being, by shooting her with a pistol.

Count two: Ronney Albert Zamora did unlawfully commit burglary of a dwelling, the property of Elinor Haggart.

Count three: Ronney Albert Zamora did unlawfully and feloniously display a certain firearm, to wit, a pistol, while committing a felony.

Count four: Ronney Albert Zamora did unlawfully by force, violence, assault, or putting in fear, take certain property, to wit, money—good and lawful currency of the United States of America; silver service; jewelry; a firearm; and an automobile, the property of Elinor Haggart, in violation of 812.13 Florida Statutes, to the evil example of all others in like cases offending, and against the peace and dignity of the State of Florida.

The people of the State of Florida has charged by indictment this defendant with those offenses. I expect to prove beyond every reasonable doubt that this defendant committed those acts, killed Elinor Haggart, had burglarized her home, stole property from her, and executed Elinor Haggart because of his fear that she would call the police. I also expect to establish beyond any reasonable doubt that at the time the defendant committed these acts, he was legally sane and should be convicted and found guilty of each and every charge.

At this point, I will advise you that due to the age of this defendant, the people of the State of Florida will not ask you for a recommendation of death upon conviction. And I will ask on behalf of the people of the State of Florida that upon your oaths as jurors, you find him guilty as charged. Thank you.

Judge Baker: Mr. Rubin.

Mr. Rubin: May it please the Court, Mr. Headley, ladies and gentlemen of the jury:

Mr. Headley has asked you to consider what he did and how he acted. The defense in this case is, why? And we're going to show you why. And we believe for the first time in this or any other jurisdiction, that your verdict is going to be unusual.

Ronney was brought to the United States by his mother at the age of four. And being a very poor girl, her very meager circumstances could not allow her to spend money for baby-sitters, nurses for this preschool-age child who spoke no English. So she plopped him down in front of a television set. And it not only became a babysitter, but it became an instructor in the English language and an instructor on the moral code of our system. And in the place of his parents or his school or his church or whatever is accepted in our society as the teacher of right and wrong and the founder of a conscience, the tube took the place of home, school, church.

. . . .

We're going to show you during the course of this trial

that Ronney Zamora was rejected almost from the moment he was conceived. Whenever he was misbehaving, his mother would tell him, "Ronney, we found you in a garbage can. Now don't bother us. Go away and watch television."

The family moved from New York because of Ronney's problems and because the father had a job offered down here. And they moved down to the rock and roll world of Miami Beach, and you will hear about the boys and the girls and their society, and what is supposed to be normal and abnormal. And it was to Miami Beach that Ronney moved next door to the woman he was to kill. And kill her he did. And we're going to show you not that he did it—we're admitting that—but why. Ronney, when he came down here, was put into this society where money talks. Status is very important. Ronney didn't have money or he didn't have the status and he couldn't keep up. So he retreated again to the world of *Baretta* and *Kojak* and *Police Woman* and *Helter Skelter*. I think that you're going to see, during this trial, perhaps for the first time in American history, the creation and destruction of a television addict.

. . . .

That is the defense in this case, that this is a documented case both before and after the shooting of an immature adolescent boy, a sociopathic personality, who at the moment of this crime could not distinguish if he was in a television play, acting it out, or whether it was cold-blooded, premeditated murder. And why would a boy do such a terrible thing to a neighbor that he liked?

That is for you to decide in this case. Thank you.

Judge Baker: Members of the jury, what counsel has said to you in their opening statements is merely an expectation of what they intend to prove and what they expect the evidence to show. It is the time when, like a road map, the attorneys attempt to guide you through the theory of their case to a conclusion which they anticipate the evidence will support.

However, this is only a theory of the case and it's not to be considered by you as evidence. The Court admonishes you that you are not to set your minds upon a determination of the issues at this time. This you will not do until you have heard all of the testimony, the argument of counsel, and the law the Court will charge you.

Reeves: The prosecution then laboriously laid out the details of crime and discovery. Zamora's confession was ignored for the moment. That was partly for the record, but partly because Thomas Headley wanted to impress the jury with the rationality of the legal and the investigative process. After all, he's going to ask these twelve people to take away most of a young man's life. The first witnesses called were the first policemen on the scene. One was Patrolman Zell Hall:

Zell Hall: . . . and from there, we detected a foul odor emitting from the house.
Thomas Headley: Did you associate that odor with anything you had smelled before?
Hall: Yes, a DOA.
Headley: And a DOA would mean what?
Hall: A dead person.

Reeves: Hall also testified that the house had been ransacked. The autopsy was performed by the Medical Examiner for Dade County, Dr. Ronald Wright:

Dr. Wright: The only really abnormal finding within the body was the presence of a gunshot wound tract which entered again the left upper abdomen, went through the area of the spleen, the diaphragm and the left lung, through the base of the heart where the major blood vessel called the inferior vena cava brings all the blood up from the lower part of the body, thence through the right lung, and exiting as indicated.
Reeves: Dr. Wright concluded that the wound was the cause

of death. A firearms specialist then testified that the bullet was a .32-calibre and that it was fired from a weapon with a six-groove left hand twist. Robert Hart:

Robert Hart: The only manufacturer of weapons with these characteristics that is encountered with any degree of frequency at all is Colt firearms.

Reeves: Mrs. Haggart's daughter, Jean Louise Moss, testified that her mother always kept at least a hundred dollars in the house. The old woman did not use credit cards. Mrs. Moss also identified the murder weapon:

Headley: Would you tell the jury, please, what she had in her possession or what type of weapon she kept?
Jean Louis Moss: It was a .32 revolver.

Reeves: The prosecutor then brought on four friends of Ronney Zamora's, four teenagers who had spent two days with him after the murder. Zamora never took the stand, so we and the jury have to see him through the eyes of other people. We've edited two hours of their testimony into five minutes here. What Thomas Headley was trying to do here was to show that Zamora acted like a normal fifteen-year-old after the murder, by implication that Ronney Zamora was legally sane, sane under the precepts of English common law, that sanity is knowing the difference between right and wrong.

Headley: (to Paul Toledo) All right—Paul, during the time that you were with Ronney, would you explain to the jury, please, his behavior, how he was acting?
Toledo: Well, he acted normal. I mean like an everyday normal kid, you know.
Headley: How do you mean by normal? What do—you know, was he doing anything strange, unusual, bizarre?
Toledo: No, he was not. You know, we all had a good time

and everything. I mean it was just like Timmy and Alan and David.
Headley: (to David Picciolo) David, did the defendant act peculiar?
Picciolo: No.
Headley: That's all the questions I have, Your Honor.
Judge Baker: Cross.
Ellis Rubin: (to Paul Toledo) Was Ronney acting normally all the time that he was with you?
Toledo: Yes, he was.
Rubin: On the trip to Disney World?
Toledo: Yes, he was.
Rubin: He was acting like all of the other fellows, right?
Toledo: Yes, he was.
Rubin: You were driving in a stolen car; you were given a ticket for speeding; a gun was pointed at you and a bullet was in it; there were girls in your room at the motel at four o'clock in the morning; Darrell told you to wipe off fingerprints from the car because it might be stolen. Is this the normal conduct of Miami Beach boys?
Thomas Headley: Objection. Argumentative, overbroad.
Judge Baker: The question is forked.

Reeves: The next witness for the State was Ronney Zamora's stepfather. Francisco Zamora testified that he had not given the boy the four hundred dollars. Then Headley continued:

Headley: Did you give the defendant a Buick automobile to drive and use around the fourth of June?
Francisco Zamora: No, sir.
Headley: Do you have any relatives, either your sister or your wife's sister, who would be the defendant's aunt, who has an automobile like that?
Zamora: No, sir.

Reeves: Then Sergeant Paul Rantanan told how Ronney

Zamora and his parents came to the Miami Beach police station. He testified that the young man was read a card describing his rights to remain silent or to consult an attorney. Sergeant Rantanan:

Paul Rantanan: He said, "I did it, and I just want to tell you about it. I want to get it off my chest."

Reeves: There were more prosecution witnesses, but we don't have time for all of them here. What we've tried to do is show how Thomas Headley presented the State's case. On the sixth day of the trial, the defense brought Zamora's mother to the stand. The defense attorney, Ellis Rubin, led Yolanda Zamora through the story of her life: her childhood in Costa Rica, the birth of the boy and the refusal of the father to marry her, then a trip to the United States, leaving the boy behind. The attempt to find a better life. The marriage to Francisco Zamora, bringing the boy north at the age of five. Ronney spoke only Spanish then. Yolanda Zamora continued:

Yolanda Zamora: The way he learned English actually was watching TV from the time he got up in the morning until he went to sleep, from the time he got here, because he came here on April and he didn't have to go to school until September.
Rubin: So who thought of television as a way to teach him English?
Mrs. Zamora: Well, there was nothing else he could do. I had to go out and work, my husband had to go out and work, and we asked this lady if she could watch him. So she would come from time to time and keep an eye on him, but it was nothing else to do.

Rubin: Did you know Mrs. Haggart who lived right next door?
Mrs. Zamora: Well, I met the lady, yes, when we moved in in February and . . .

Rubin: So you were there about five months?
Mrs. Zamora: We were there from February the twenty-seventh, yes, we move in there.
Rubin: Did you talk to her?
Mrs. Zamora: Sometimes we say good morning and hello, but that was about it.
Rubin: Did Ronney ever talk to her?
Mrs. Zamora: Yes, yes. Sometimes we were fixing the yard, the three of us, my husband, Ronney, and myself. And she would come close to the fence and tell us what a good boy he was, and what a nice family we were and we are.

Reeves: That was the most solid evidence presented about Ronney Zamora's television viewing habits. Prosecutor Headley chose not to cross examine Mrs. Zamora. She was obviously a sympathetic witness. And he also avoided any repetitive emphasis on the television watching defense. Defense Attorney Rubin then called a series of psychiatrists and psychologists. He tried to develop the argument here that violence on television could twist the mind of a fifteen-year-old. Ellis Rubin examines Dr. Walter Reid:

Dr. Reid: I found him to be a boy of a little above average intelligence. He seems to have the kind of ability necessary to make it in school, if he's interested in what he's doing. In terms of personality, I saw somebody who is a fairly classical sociopathic personality.
Rubin: All right. Stop right there. What do those words mean? What is a sociopathic personality?
Dr. Reid: Sociopathic personality is a psychiatric term that denotes a person who is emotionally cool, calloused, has little in the way of remorse or guilt, has little or no ability to feel for other people, and otherwise presents pretty much as a normal person.
Rubin: Doctor, within a reasonable psychological certainty, how does a person become a sociopathic personality?

Dr. Reid: The current theories say that it has to do with inconsistent parenting during early childhood. It has to do with, if you want, loose standards, double standards. It has to do with parents not providing the kind of appropriate punishment and guidance for a child early in life.
Rubin: Does a person deliberately become a sociopathic personality, or does it just happen?
Dr. Reid: It just happens.

Reeves: Assistant State Attorney Richard Katz cross examines:

Richard Katz: Doctor, you essentially found, in your evaluation of Ronney Zamora, that Ronney Zamora is a sociopath, is that correct?
Dr. Reid: Correct.
Katz: Mr. Rubin didn't ask you, but did you make some determination . . .
Rubin: One moment, please. Your Honor, I think that's an improper predicate for a question. It's directed at me more than it is at the doctor.
Judge Baker: All right. Forget it.
Rubin: There's a lot of things I couldn't ask him.
Katz: I'll rephrase the question, Your Honor.
Judge Baker: Please do.
Katz: Did you make a finding as to whether or not Ronney Zamora knew right from wrong at the time he shot Elinor Haggart?
Dr. Reid: Yes.
Katz: And what was your finding?
Dr. Reid: I think he can distinguish right from wrong.
Katz: Isn't it true that the classic definition of a sociopath is that a sociopath knows right from wrong, but doesn't care?
Dr. Reid: That's one of the criteria.
Katz: Sometimes that's been called moral insanity, isn't that correct?
Dr. Reid: Right. Correct.

Katz: And when you stated that Ronney Zamora perhaps automatically reacted in disregard of what he knew was wrong—it's automatic in the sense that he couldn't cure himself on the spot of being a sociopath, someone who didn't care about what was wrong. Isn't that true?
Dr. Reid: That's true.
Katz: Is there any doubt in your mind that Ronney Zamora knew when he pulled the trigger on the gun, it would, in fact, project a bullet which would kill Elinor Haggart?
Dr. Reid: I feel sure of it.

Reeves: So Ronney Zamora is characterized as a sociopathic personality—but not insane. The testimony is that the defendant knew right from wrong, that he understood the consequences of his act. Another witness, a psychiatrist, describes sociopaths as con-artists, liars, cheaters, and thieves—but not insane.

Rubin: What is your name and address?
Dr. Thomas: Margaret Hanratty Thomas. (she states her address)
Rubin: What is your occupation or profession?
Dr. Thomas: Psychologist and college professor.
Rubin: Are you prepared to say that an excessive amount of television viewing would have an effect on an emotionally disturbed fifteen-year-old male child from a middle class, poor economic background?
Dr. Thomas: It's very possible.
Rubin: Very possible? Can you say it within a reasonable psychological certainty?
Dr. Thomas: I would feel fairly confident that, given that type of background, an excessive amount of television violence would—well, it has an effect on everyone. It would be much more likely to have an unusual or extreme effect on such a child, in my opinion.
Rubin: (to Judge Baker) You may inquire.

Judge Baker: Let me ask you this. Can you state, within reasonable psychological certainty, under the set of facts that Mr. Rubin just gave you, that such an amount of television on the type of child could produce . . .
Rubin: Your Honor, I should have added six to eight hours a day, as has been testified. I'm sorry. I didn't put that in.
Judge Baker: Whatever—could produce a state of mind where he did not know right from wrong and could not appreciate the nature and consequences of his acts?
Dr. Thomas: Watching that much television over a long period of time, in my opinion, is at least one of the important factors as to how a person acquires a sense of right and wrong.
Judge Baker: That's not the question. The question is can you state, with reasonable psychological certainty, in any of the tests that you've conducted, in any of the tests that you have referred to, in any of the papers that you've published—not that it could—that it has—had that effect on any individual tested, to the extent that they did not know right from wrong?
Dr. Thomas: Would studies that show that children who tend to watch a lot of violent television tend to be more approving . . .
Judge Baker: No. Not approving. Would they be so affected that they would not know right from wrong and appreciate the nature and consequences of their act—in other words, have absolutely no idea of right or wrong, couldn't appreciate the nature and consequences of their act? In other words, are you familiar with the rule of M'Naghten's case?
Dr. Thomas: Well, I learned of it last evening when Mr. Headley was taking my deposition, and I guess I'm a little confused.
Headley: Judge, excuse me.
Dr. Thomas: What I'm saying is . . .
Headley: May I ask a question, Your Honor?
Judge Baker: Please.
Rubin: Your Honor, she's answering your questions.
Judge Baker: Let her answer mine. Then you can ask one. But just please let me finish. Go ahead.
Headley: I'm sorry.

Dr. Thomas: The distinction that I'm having trouble with is that, yes, I would feel comfortable saying that exposure to television violence can shape a child's conceptions of what is right and wrong—that is such that a very heavy television viewer, perhaps, who comes up in an atmosphere where there are not other restraints built in can—could develop such an attitude that what society in general sees as right and wrong is not his reality, is not his sense of right and wrong. You see what I mean, that it's all—for example, there are studies that show that children tend to think of aggression as more ordinary, more commonplace, and approve of it more as a result of exposure to television violence. Their sense of right and wrong then, is a little different than that of a child who watches very little television. They do have it. I mean, I guess those values are different.

Judge Baker: I'll accept that values are different. But we're talking about the legal definition of insanity, which—go ahead, Mr. Headley. Ask your question. Maybe it'll clear it up.

Headley: Dr. Thomas, can you advise the Court of one study or one experiment or any number that have linked the viewing of television violence with insanity?

Dr. Thomas: You mean use the term "insanity"?

Headley: Yes.

Dr. Thomas: Legal insanity—of course not.

Headley: I think that's all we're resolving here, Your Honor.

Judge Baker: That's it.

Rubin: One more chance. They're comparing apples and oranges. How can you relate, Your Honor, psychological, medical, scientific experiments of proof with the legal definition of the word "insanity"? This is not her field. Our field is the legal definition of a defense. Her field is what are the effects of television violence on children. Your Honor will instruct the jury on the law of insanity. I want to show the jury the facts that went into this child's concept of right and wrong. Your Honor, she's prepared to—I have psychiatrists who will

use this testimony, subject to cross examination, who will testify as to what you asked this young doctor. She can't testify that there's ever been a case where insanity has been found to result from too much television, because they don't have the word "insanity" in her field. They don't have it even in the field of psychiatry, as you know.
Judge Baker: I understand that.
Rubin: Let the scientists come—let the psychiatrists, Your Honor, come in. And let Your Honor voir dire the psychiatrists and say, "Has there ever been a case where too much television has caused insanity?" And they will answer, "Yes." And the victim is Ronney Zamora. And let the jury hear that. Please.
Judge Baker: Let me ask you this, ma'am. Let's forget the word "insanity." In any of your tests, in any scientific journal that you have read, have you ever conclusively linked any particular television program or amount of television violence directly to a homicide?
Dr. Thomas: Well, those are not scientific studies. There are cases . . .
Judge Baker: Or any crime?
Dr. Thomas: No, because they're always after the fact. You can't . . .
Judge Baker: Thank you. The testimony is excluded.

Reeves: Ellis Rubin has lost. Judge Baker ruled that television watching was not pertinent to Ronney Zamora's case. The jury didn't hear any of this. They were sequestered in the jury room.

Reeves: The next morning, we hear from a psychologist who interviewed Ronney Zamora and his mother. Dr. Helen Ackerman was cross examined by Richard Katz.

Richard Katz: Doctor, it would be fair to say, would it not, that psychologists know very much about the generalities of how people learn and what causes people to develop from infants to mature adults. Isn't that true?

Dr. Helen Ackerman: That's true, you could say that.

Katz: But all the knowledge that doctors know, doctors have not been able to pinpoint what factors specifically cause certain people to commit crimes. Isn't that true?

Dr. Ackerman: No, that's not true. If you look at the work, for example, of Kellegeracas * or Bender—these are people who are authorities in, say, adolescents who commit homicide. They can pretty well tell you the factors that are involved in creating a youngster that will commit a homicidal act, if that's what you are asking me.

Katz: They know generalities of certain types of people who commit crimes, some of the things that are in common in their background. Isn't that true?

Dr. Ackerman: They know specific things that are in their background.

Katz: Such as?

Dr. Ackerman: Such as a punitive father, for example. A background where an individual is punished very severely by the parents; a background where a youngster does not know how to express aggression in a socially acceptable way; a background that is very poor in affection, and, you know, tender loving care. These are pretty specific things; they're not just pie in the sky.

Katz: And these things which may in general lead people to commit crimes, do criminal acts, do acts against other people—these are matters which have not necessarily been linked with sanity. Isn't that true?

Dr. Ackerman: Well, you're asking me about a legal definition of sanity and I'm not going to get into that.

Katz: That's because psychologists have been unable to link these factors with insanity. Isn't that true?

*correct spelling uncertain

Dr. Ackerman: Well, that's your statement. I disagree with it, but you're entitled to have that statement as yours.

Katz: Well, it's true that psychologists don't have a crystal ball. They can't look into a crystal ball and determine what someone's state of mind was sometime back in time. Isn't that true?

Dr. Ackerman: That's true for all of us, yes.

Katz: Thank you.

Judge Baker: Redirect.

Ellis Rubin: Now, you answered a question on cross examination of the factors that go into aggression?

Dr. Ackerman: Producing a youngster that can commit homicide, yes.

Rubin: Is television one of those factors?

Katz: Objection.

Rubin: He opened it.

Judge Baker: Overruled.

Rubin: Thank you, Your Honor.

Dr. Ackerman: It has been mentioned as a factor, a possible factor.

Rubin: Where has it been mentioned?

Katz: Objection. There are many things that are possible in the world.

Rubin: And he asked them.

Judge Baker: Let's rephrase the questions to within a psychological certainty.

Rubin: Yes, Your Honor. (to Dr. Ackerman) Are there any studies that have been done by recognized scientists and psychologists that have concluded within a reasonable psychological certainty that a sociopathic boy from a poor to middle class background seeing six to eight hours of television a day from the age of five until fifteen is likely to imitate the violence that he sees, and is likely to form his standards of conduct from those television hours?

Katz: Objection to the form of the question, Your Honor, as

to what someone's likely to do. Furthermore, I would cite that the hypothet goes beyond the facts which are in evidence.
Judge Baker: I don't think that's accurate. You can ask if she can answer that within reasonable psychological certainty.
Rubin: I believe I did put that premise in, but I will ask again. (to Dr. Ackerman) Can you answer that from a reasonable psychological certainty?
Dr. Ackerman: I am not sure what the question was to begin with, but all these factors . . .
Rubin: Can you answer first of all?
Dr. Ackerman: Oh. Repeat it again.
Rubin: (to Court Reporter) Would you please read the question?

(Court Reporter reads back question)
Dr. Ackerman: I would say . . .
Katz: Objection, this time, because it asks for what he's likely to do, not what someone will do. There is no direct cause and effect.
Judge Baker: The question was within reasonable psychological certainty. If she can answer, I'll let her.
Rubin: Would you answer, please, Doctor?
Dr. Ackerman: Okay, there are no actual studies per se, but this would mean the individual would be a high risk person, in terms of being exposed to this kind of material.
Katz: Objection, and ask that the Court strike the answer.
Judge Baker: Sustained. The answer should be stricken. If there are no studies, then it's just an off-the-cuff opinion. That's way outside of what's acceptable.
Rubin: Is there such a study that says that this type of a child is a high risk . . .
Dr. Ackerman: Yes.
Rubin: . . . and likely to engage in aggressive conduct?
Katz: Objection, leading.
Judge Baker: Overruled.
Rubin: Is there?

Dr. Ackerman: Yes. Yes.
Rubin: That says he's a high risk? Do you have that study?
Dr. Ackerman: Okay.
Rubin: Would you please find it? I just want . . .
Katz: Objection. This subject is totally inadmissible.
Judge Baker: It is speculation. I will not allow the study to be admitted into evidence or any reference made to it.
Rubin: All right, Your Honor.

Reeves: The question is whether he knew the nature and consequence of his actions. Rubin questioned Psychiatrist Michael Gilbert:

Rubin: Doctor, what are the bad effects of the television violence?
Dr. Michael Gilbert: Well, it gives a distorted sense of values. For example, it has been demonstrated that the average child watches thousands of killings on TV. Now, a child like Ronney Zamora, maybe sees five or ten times that many killings. When one has seen that many killings, the death of a human being in that type of situation is no more significant than swatting a fly. This develops a concept, an attitude, a distortion of reality, if you will, that the shooting of a person is of no greater consequence, let us say, than the swatting of a fly.

Now, the reason is, you see, if a shooting in television were accompanied by the physical agony of the person who's shot, the bleeding and suffering, and we're also showed the funeral, and also showed the suffering of this person's family, his children or his parents or what have you, all as a consequence of this shooting, as contrasted when, "Bang, bang," and the scene goes on. They don't look to see if the person is alive or dead or still bleeding or he can be saved or whatever. And then he gets a distorted concept of what television death is, what death by shooting is, whereas if he saw all these other things which are reality, then he has a realistic concept of what death is. But this, then, gives him an unrealistic concept of what a death by shooting is. It's not real; it's distorted. And this is what happens in the case of an adolescent in Ronney Zamora's situation.

Rubin: Did it have anything to do with the shooting of Elinor Haggart?

Dr. Gilbert: It certainly did.

Rubin: Can you explain that, please?

Dr. Gilbert: From the material I obtained—I verified it every way—best way I could. Prior to the shooting, this boy knew it was wrong to kill Mrs. Haggart. He had described to me an argument he had with his accomplice, if you want to call him that, this companion, where this fellow had suggested to him that he put a pillow over the gun and muffle it and shoot her, and he said, "No way, there's no way I could do it. I won't do it."

He described some polemics, an argument or a discussion that went on with Agrella in which Agrella pointed out, "Look, after all, I am the one who's robbing all the silverware and lugging out the television and doing all this, and you got to do something. So you shoot her, as your contribution . . ." to this caper or whatever it was.

Now, he expresses very firmly, very definitively, "That's not right. I don't want to kill her. I would not kill her."

Now, at the time he first gets the gun, this to him is not a weapon; it's a play toy, because he describes he opened the barrel, he spun it around, he waved it here, he pointed it there, pointed it here, put the barrel in his mouth and had some fantasies about whatever he did which led to putting the gun in his mouth, aimed it at Mrs. Zamora, (sic) aimed it at the ceiling, aimed it at various things. He was playing a game with a toy.

Now then, Mrs. Haggart makes a statement to the boys, she says she knows he's the next-door neighbor and she is going to tell the police. It is that point that Ronney told me

the gun went off accidentally. Now, as I indicated before, accidents don't just happen; there's a reason for accidents happening. Now then, if this child has been exposed to thousands and thousands of situations where he has seen, when you are threatened, bang, you shoot. You take this emotionally disturbed child in a situation which is foreign to him—he's never been a robber before; he's never held a gun in his hand before—but he has been conditioned that the proper thing or the thing to do is to shoot. He has no conscious awareness, intention, volition, if you will, of what he is doing, but the trigger finger reflexly contracts over the trigger and the gun goes off.
Rubin: Doctor, did you form an opinion within a reasonable medical certainty as to the mental condition of Ronney Zamora on June fourth, 1977, at the time he fired a gun at Mrs. Haggart?
Dr. Gilbert: Yes, I have.
Rubin: What is that opinion?
Dr. Gilbert: That up to that time he knew the difference between right and wrong. At the time of the shooting, he did not know what he was doing. Therefore, he could not know the nature and consequence of his act, since he did not know what he was doing, and therefore, he can't—couldn't judge that what he was doing was wrong.
Judge Baker: All right. Cross examination, Mr. Headley.
Thomas Headley: Dr. Gilbert, first I expect that this is going to be very short. I would ask, Dr. Gilbert, that in response to my questions, you try as best you can to use layman's terminology. I know it may be difficult, but I'll try to keep the questions simple.

I believe you testified that when the defendant pulled the trigger, this was an unconscious conditioned reflex. Is that your terminology?
Dr. Gilbert: By definition, a conditioned reflex is unconscious.
Headley: So it was a conditioned reflex that caused the defendant to shoot Mrs. Haggart, in your opinion.

Dr. Gilbert: That is—yes.

Headley: The defendant tells you that it was an accident. Is that true?

Dr. Gilbert: That is correct.

Headley: After examining him, you don't accept his account that it's an accident, but find that it was a result of a conditioned reflex.

Dr. Gilbert: That is correct.

Headley: In order for there to be a conditioned reflex, isn't it true that you must be conditioned by something?

Dr. Gilbert: That is correct.

Headley: And I believe you testified during direct examination that this defendant was conditioned by his exposure to television. Is that correct, sir?

Dr. Gilbert: By his excessive exposure to television.

Headley: Is it true, Dr. Gilbert, that you believe, in your opinion, the defendant was legally sane when he entered the home of Mrs. Haggart?

Dr. Gilbert: Yes.

Headley: And that he was sane all that time, all—up until the moment of the shot? I'm not trying to play games or do something tricky here. He's sane while he's sitting there in the living room watching Mrs. Haggart?

Dr. Gilbert: Legally sane as we have defined it here.

Headley: He knows right from wrong. He knows it would be bad to kill Mrs. Haggart.

Dr. Gilbert: That is correct.

Headley: And isn't it true that Darrel Agrella, according to what the defendant told you, suggested that the defendant shoot her and kill her at that point, but he said no?

Dr. Gilbert: That is correct.

Headley: And the reason he would say no at that time is because he knew it was wrong to kill her. Is that correct?

Dr. Gilbert: That is correct.

Headley: Now, when it comes right to the moment that the

gun is shot, is it your opinion that the defendant went from sane to insane and back to sane in a matter of two or three seconds?

Dr. Gilbert: That is correct.

Headley: Now, the exact time—which we can't reconstruct—but would the time period be from when the trigger was pulled until he heard the noise and this brought him back to his senses?

Dr. Gilbert: More or less.

Headley: This then could be no more than a second.

Dr. Gilbert: Second or seconds. I think by the time the noise subsides and one gets his faculties back where he can look around and see what happens. Probably—let us say a few seconds, but I think we're really pulling at hairs here. A second, a few seconds or ten seconds. I don't think it's of any great consequence.

Headley: Okay. Considering the legal sense of the word "sanity," did he, in your opinion, continue to be sane after Mrs. Haggart was shot, the property was removed from the house, and he went to Disney World?

Dr. Gilbert: There was—not completely. There was an impairment there, of the extent of his so-called sanity there.

Headley: When?

Dr. Gilbert: All during those next few days when he went up to Disney World and his conduct after that, until such time as he was apprehended.

Headley: So in your opinion, he was legally insane while he was in Disney World with his friends?

Dr. Gilbert: Let me repeat. I said there is an impairment.

Headley: An impairment. But Dr. Gilbert, it's important in a court of law that we deal with legal insanity. Do you feel that he was legally insane while he was in Disney World with his friends?

Dr. Gilbert: I think I've answered the questions to the best of my ability. For me to make an all-or-nothing answer to something where there's a very significant quantitative difference makes me say something that I don't mean.

Headley: Well, Dr. Gilbert, unfortunately you have to do that, sir. Now, he's either sane or insane in the legal sense. Now, in your opinion, as best you can form it, was he sane or insane while he was in Orlando?

Dr. Gilbert: I don't know how I can answer that, other than to say that there was an impairment of his sanity. Now, at what point does one make a completely qualitative distinction between something which is quantitatively different is—I certainly have to think about a little, because it's forced me—this question is forcing me into an artificial construct. It's almost like saying how high is up.

Reeves: Rubin continued the same lines of inquiry with other psychiatrists.

Dr. William Corwin: He knew that he had done something wrong. He admitted that.
Ellis Rubin: Did he admit that he knew what he had done both before and after he did it?
Dr. Corwin: Yes, he was quite aware of the circumstances.
Rubin: Is that in your report, that he realized what he had done after he did it?
Dr. Corwin: Yes, he knew that he had shot her.
Rubin: Did he realize that he had done it?
Dr. Corwin: Yes, he realized it.

Reeves: Dr. Jaslow:

Dr. Albert Jaslow: Even though there were a conditioned reflex, especially in the human, there is still understanding and awareness of what's happening.

Reeves: Dr. Corwin:

Dr. William Corwin: It is completely unlikely that in the space of a brief period, like on to two or three or four or five seconds, the time in which it would take to pull a trigger, which, in itself, requires some effort and conscious volition, it is completely unlikely that he would be, at that moment, legally insane.

Reeves: That was the end of testimony in the murder case of Ronney Zamora. Under Florida law, the first closing argument was given by the prosecution, in this case, Richard Katz. Ellis Rubin then offered his closing argument for the defense. Then Thomas Headley concluded with a prosecution rebuttal. We begin with Katz:

Judge Baker: All right, Mr. Katz. You may begin your closing argument.
Richard Katz: May it please the Court, Mr. Rubin, ladies and gentlemen:

We're nearing the end of the trial, and it's my pleasure at this time on behalf of the State of Florida, Mr. Headley, and myself, to thank all of you for about the last ten days or so of patience, in and out of the jury room, back and forth from your hotel.

I'm going to have an opportunity to address you and make closing remarks. The procedure that's followed is then Mr. Rubin will have an opportunity on behalf of the defendant to have his turn to address you, and then the State will have a period of time for rebuttal. And Mr. Headley will give you that rebuttal argument. And following all the argument, tomorrow morning, the Court, Judge Baker, will charge you, will give you the law which you are to follow when you resolve the issues in this case.

The State has proven, and the defense admitted that the defendant, Ronney Zamora, participated in the burglary of Elinor Haggart's home. The defense has admitted that Mrs.

Haggart came home during the course of the burglary and discovered the defendant. Furthermore, the defense admitted that Ronney Zamora possessed a firearm while engaged in the commission of a felony. We needn't really go into those areas at length. It boils down substantially, to the area of sanity. And even there, we can boil that down, because the defense—there was only one witness, whether a lay witness or a psychiatrist or a psychologist—the only witness who has said that Ronney Zamora was insane at any time was Dr. Michael Gilbert. And he limited it to a very short period of time. If you recall his testimony last night, he said one second, three seconds, five seconds, ten seconds, it's really like pulling hair. A very short period of time, a matter of several seconds. His sanity is only at issue during that period of time.

Thank you very much . . .

Judge Baker: (to Ellis Rubin) All right. You may proceed.
Ellis Rubin: Ladies and gentlemen of the jury:

This building, this courtroom, is our temple of justice. All rights, all responsibilities, life and sometimes death, flow from this building. And so will your verdict.

Naturally, I'm fighting for Ronney Zamora. Of course, Ronney knew right from wrong, but I don't think that any doctor has told you that he wasn't a sociopathic personality who could not refrain from doing wrong, and he didn't care whether he did wrong. And from thousands and thousands and thousands of murders that he has seen, this was a reaction that he imitated, or a conditioned reflex. I'm not concerned with those scientific words. You and I are going to talk common sense. I couldn't understand half of what these doctors were talking about. That's why they're experts and they want to make us experts, because you're going to go in that little room, you're going to have to tell which psychiatrist was guessing correctly. It's a heavy burden.

It's almost six o'clock. Normally, that is supper time. But

there are millions of people who don't eat supper at six o'clock anymore, because that's the time for the news on television. You see, television can change our habits. It used to be that people went to bed when the sun went down and got up when the sun got up. And then into the nineteenth century and the twentieth century, the Industrial Revolution and modern civilization and all of the conveniences that you and I enjoy. In the 1940's and '50's, along came this movie set in your own home. Why? So they started to produce programs which would draw attention and viewers, because the more viewers you get, the more the producer of the program can charge the sponsors of the products that are advertised. So our sleeping habits started changing too. Television has changed when we eat and when we sleep and when we kill and when we don't kill, and how to kill, and the good guys can kill, and the bad guys can kill, and it all comes on the tube again next week, same time, same station. And we're getting so civilized now and so sophisticated and so great in our wealth and in our luxury that they even have murder and rape on giant screens in your own home, and that isn't good enough. Now, they've invented a machine that, in case there's a murder on one channel, and you want to see a rape on another channel, you can hook up this machine, and it records the channel that you're not watching, so that when you're not saturated with the murder, that isn't good enough, you can then go in your bedroom and hook up this machine and see the rape also. You don't miss a thing.

It's time we did something. It's time we did something for Elinor Haggart. Your verdict which says that Ronney Zamora is not guilty by reason of insanity—because if he were to be guilty of murder, television would be an accessory to the crime—your verdict is going to say this woman's life was not taken in vain, because your verdict is the day that it began to stop.

Thank you very much.

Judge Baker: Mr. Headley, you may close.

Thomas Headley: If it please the Court, Mr. Rubin, members of the jury:

The hour is late. After two weeks, I'm exhausted. I'm certain that you are, as well.

Now, as I listened to Mr. Rubin, it struck me that this defense fits this defendant like a glove, because it cannot accept responsibility, just as a sociopath cannot accept responsibility. It must place the blame someplace else. It must point the finger someplace else. And where is the finger pointed? At television; at Darrell Agrella; at the Miami Beach Police Department; at the teenagers on Miami Beach—every place but where it belongs—right on that defendant. And it may have come across your minds as you sat and listened to the testimony in this case, why did we go through all of those days of presenting each witness and each bit of testimony and each bit of evidence, when Mr. Rubin, in his opening statement, acknowledged and admitted that this defendant was in the home of Elinor Haggart, and, in fact, that this defendant even shot her? Well, I suggest to you that the State of Florida had the obligation and the responsibility to convince you beyond every reasonable doubt that the defendant was guilty, and that he was sane when he committed these acts.

How nice it would be if we didn't know that Elinor Haggart was shot in her own home. How nice it would be if you didn't know that Elinor Haggart was an eighty-three-year-old woman unable to protect herself. Mr. Rubin asked that you make a martyr of her and find the person that killed her not guilty. So what does he do? The only thing he can do: "It was an accident. I had never had a gun before. I didn't know how to use the gun. I was sticking it in my ear, in my mouth."

The whole case depends on Dr. Gilbert. You heard his testimony. I didn't understand too much of it, to be honest with you. But I got from it that he's selling a defense. He is attempting to sell to you that this defendant was insane and he says that his opinion is based within a reasonable medical certainty. And then I asked Dr. Gilbert, "Will you explain that to me, please, sir?"

And he hemmed and he hawed and he used these big words. And then he finally said if the state of our scientific knowledge indicates that something could happen once in a *million* times—*once* in a million times—"I would consider that to be within reasonable medical probability."

I suggest that the testimony offered by Dr. Gilbert is something that if you were at a friend's house, you would listen to politely for a few minutes and then throw up your hands and say, "Nonsense. Nonsense."

I asked you during voir dire examination if you could try this defendant, and I asked if you could look him in the eye, try him as any other defendant. He's young, but he was old enough to kill. And I suggest that he must be held accountable and responsible for his acts. The defendant is guilty. He's been proven guilty beyond all reasonable doubt, and his sanity at the time he shot and killed Elinor Haggart has been established beyond all reasonable doubt. I ask in behalf of the people of the State of Florida, that your verdict speak the truth, that you find this defendant guilty as charged.

Thank you.

Judge Baker: Ladies and gentlemen of the jury, you may take with you into the jury room the same everyday common sense, together with your knowledge of men and affairs that you brought with you into this courtroom. Consider and deliberate. Let your verdict be dated. Close with the words, "So say we all." Be signed by one of your number as a foreperson. And speak the truth as you find it.

Judge Baker: You may be seated, gentlemen. Mr. Foreman, has the jury reached a verdict?
John Katab: Yes, we have, Your Honor.
Judge Baker: Hand it to the clerk, please.

The defendant will rise. Publish the verdict.

The Clerk: Circuit Court of the Eleventh Judicial Circuit of Florida, in and for Dade County, case number 77-25123 A, the State of Florida versus Ronney Albert Zamora. Verdict: We, the jury, at Miami, Dade County, Florida, this sixth day of October, A.D. 1977, find the defendant, Ronney Albert Zamora, as to count one of the indictment, guilty of murder in the first degree. So say we all, N. John Katab, foreman . . .

(Clerk continues to read verdict as
Reeves' voice is heard)

Reeves: The jury had been out for only two hours. They also found Ronney Zamora guilty of charges of burglary, armed robbery, and possession of a weapon. Each juror then swore that he or she agreed with the guilty verdict.

(clerk names the jurors, who respond
yes to the guilty verdict)

Judge Baker: The jurors having acceded in the verdict, the defendant having been found guilty by a jury of murder in the first degree is adjudicated by the Court guilty of murder in the first degree.

The jury having found the defendant guilty of burglary is adjudicated guilty by the Court of burglary.

The jury having found the defendant guilty of possession of a weapon while in the commission of an offense is adjudicated guilty by the Court.

The jury having found the defendant guilty of armed robbery is adjudicated guilty by the Court.

Sentencing will be set Monday, November the seventh, at nine A.M. . . .

(to Ronney Zamora) Is there anything you want to say before this Court passes sentence?

Ronney Zamora: No, sir.

Judge Baker: All right. The adjudicated has been entered.

As to count one: The statute leaves no alternative than sentencing as an adult, having been tried as an adult. It is the sentence of this Court that you be confined in the State Department of Corrections for the remainder of your natural life, without parole for a term of twenty-five years.

As to count two: Concurrently with count one, it is the sentence of this Court that you be confined in the State Department of Corrections for the term of twenty-five years.

As to count three: Concurrently with the sentences heretofore imposed on counts one and two, it is the sentence of this Court that you be confined in the State Department of Corrections for a term of three years.

As to count four: Concurrently with the sentences heretofore imposed on counts one and two, it is the sentence of this tence of this Court that you be confined in the State Penitentiary for a term of twenty-five years.

The Court includes and recommends to the Director of the Department of Corrections that you be placed in a youthful offender facility and that you further be given the benefit of whatever psychiatric, psychological care is available within the State Department of Corrections, and if that is insufficient, to report back to this Court, at which time we will attempt to make some other arrangement.

All right. The Court will be in recess for five minutes.

INDEX

Anglo-Saxon peoples, 59
Arraignment, 29, 31–33, 75
Arrest, 6, 13, 25–27, 52
Attica Prison, 68
Auburn system, 66–67

Bail, 27
Banishment, 58, 61, 65
Bazelon, David, 51
Beccaria, Cesare, 64
Bill of Rights, 24
Blacks, 13–14, 68, 77
Block watches, 71–72, 74
Boland, Barbara, 48
Brain damage, 9
Burglary, 71, 72, 75

Capital punishment, 59–61
Career criminals, 3–4

Causes of crime, 7–15, 41
Cherry Hill Penitentiary, 66
Citizen action, 69–78
Civilian patrols, 74
Colonial America, 65
Community Crime Prevention Program, 74–75
Compensation, 59–61
Confessions, 25–26
Corporal punishment, 59–61, 63, 65, 66
Counseling, 65, 67
Court watching, 73–74
Courts, 18–20, 29–39, 60
Creative sentencing, 53–55
Cressey, Donald R., 52–53
Crime blockers, 74
Criminal Personality, 3–4
Criminals, 1–6, 48–49

Crowding, 28, 30, 45–47, 67
C type criminal, 3–4

Depression, 12–13
Deterrence, 41, 47, 49, 51, 60, 61, 64, 65
Devil's Island, 62
Di Grazia, Robert, 76
Drawing and quartering, 61
Due process, 24

England, 38, 59–62, 64, 65
Ex-convicts, 43, 55–56, 75

Fear, 14, 18, 51–52, 70
Federal courts, 35, 36
Federal Criminal Code, 46
Feuds, 59
Fines, 42, 44, 60, 61, 65
Fleming, Macklin, 49
Foucault, Michel, 63–64
Fourth Amendment, 26
Freemen, 59, 60
French Guiana, 62

Germanic peoples, 59
Governor's Commission on Administration of Justice, 75
Grand jury, 28–29
Guilt, 10, 24, 25, 29–30, 50, 52
Gun control laws, 76, 77

Hand, Learned, 51
Handguns, 76–77
Hanging, 61, 65
Head injury, 9
Heredity, 9–10
Hillsboro, New Hampshire, 55

Insanity pleas, 38–39
Internal theories of crime, 7–8
Interpretation of law, 4
Isolation, 49, 64–66

Jail, 27, 28, 50, 55, 65, 73
Judges, 20, 28–34, 36, 39, 44–47, 51, 54
Jury, 27–30, 34, 36, 38, 39

Kennedy, Edward M., 46
Kings, 60, 63

Law Enforcement Assistance Administration, 41, 74
Laws, 4, 45, 47, 59
Lawyers, 27, 45
Lee, Wilbert, 36–37
Lex talionis, 58–59
Locks, 71
Lombroso, Cesare, 7

Maximum security prison, 67
McKay, Robert, 41
Menninger, Karl, 50–51

Miranda decision, 25–26
M'Naghten Rule, 38
Murder, 21–23, 51–52, 76–77

National Criminal Justice Reference Service, 77–78
National Neighborhood Watch, 71–72
North Carolina, 44–45

Operation ID, 71
OR, 27–28

Parole, 42–44, 47, 53, 75
Parole board, 42–47, 67–68
Penal colonies, 62
Penal reform, 51, 63–65
Penal servitude, 64–67
Penitentiaries, 64–66
Pennsylvania prison system, 65–66
Pitts, Freddie, 36–37
Plea bargaining, 30–31, 40
Pleas, 29–30
Police, 18, 22–23, 25–26, 71–76
Poverty, 12–13
Prevention, 41, 42, 52–53
    citizen action, 69–78
Prison, 41, 44, 47–50, 52, 54–56
    discipline, 42, 46, 66
    history, 62–68
    lockstep, 66

reform, 67–68
riots, 67, 68
ships, 61–62
Private crimes, 58
Property marking, 71, 74
Prosecuting attorney, 29, 34, 36, 39, 47
Psychological theories, 10–12
Psychopaths, 10–11
Psychotherapy, 67
Public crimes, 58, 60
Public executions, 61, 63
Public humiliation, 58, 61, 65
Public Image of Courts, 19–20
Punishment, 10–11, 41, 42, 49–52
    history, 57–68

Quakers, 65

Racial hostilities, 68
Rape, 12, 20–21, 76
Rasphuis of Amsterdam, 64
Reasonable cause, 26, 29
Recidivism, 68
Rehabilitation, 28, 46, 49, 50, 54, 65, 67–68
Repeat offenders, 43–44, 48
Reporting crime, 16–23, 72–75
Restitution, 54–55, 75
Revenge, 12, 50–52, 58–60, 63

Role models, 14

St. Louis Women's Crusade Against Crime, 73–74
Samenow, Stanton, 3
Saudi Arabia, 51, 57
Scoppetta, Nicholas, 48
Sentences, 4, 39–42, 44–50, 53–55, 75
Serious crime, 6, 13, 20, 48–49, 51–52, 60, 77
Silberman, Charles E., 13–14, 46
Silence, 65–67
Sixth Amendment, 27
Slaves, 59, 60
Social control, 52, 57–58
Social pressures, 13
Sociological theories, 12–14
Solitary confinement, 65, 66
Solving crimes, 21–23, 75
Solzhenitsyn, Alexander, 62
Soviet Union, 62
Speck, Richard, 9
State Courts, National Center of, 19–20
Street crimes: *See* Serious crimes

Thrill-seeking, 11
Torture, 57, 60–61, 63, 66
Trials, 27–30, 32–39, 74
  TV on Trial, 37–38, 82–113
Tribal societies, 58

TV on Trial, 37–38, 82–113

United States Congress, 46, 77
United States Supreme Court, 25, 26, 31

Vera Institute of Justice, 18–19
Victimless crimes, 75
Victims, 12, 40, 51, 54, 72, 75, 76
Victim-witness assistance programs, 19, 73
Violent crimes: *See* Serious crimes
Vocational training, 67
Volunteers, 73–74

Whistlestop, 72, 73
White collar crime, 14
Wilson, James Q., 49
Witnesses, 17–19, 21, 22, 72, 73, 75
Wolfgang, Marvin, 5
Work, 64–67
Workhouses, 64
Work-release, 53

XYY and XXY chromosome syndrome, 7–8

Yochelson, Samuel, 3
Yukl, Charles, 43–44

Zamora, Ronney, 37–38, 82–113